Building AI Pipelines with LangGraph & LangChain

A Developer's Guide to Building, Scaling, and Automating AI

By

Nathan Steele

Contents

Part 1: Foundations of AI Workflow Automation

Chapter 1: Introduction to AI Workflow Automation

1.1 What is an AI Workflow?

Understanding AI Workflows

Artificial Intelligence (AI) workflows define the structured sequence of operations that drive AI-powered systems. They serve as **the backbone of modern AI applications**, ensuring smooth data flow, model execution, decision-making, and automation. Unlike traditional software workflows, which operate on predefined rules, AI workflows involve **dynamic, adaptive, and data-driven decision-making**.

An AI workflow encompasses **data processing, model training, inference, and automation**, enabling intelligent decision-making at scale. These workflows power **recommendation systems, fraud detection, AI-driven customer support, and autonomous agents**, making them essential for businesses aiming to leverage AI for operational efficiency and innovation.

The Evolution of AI Workflows

Early AI systems relied on **monolithic, rule-based architectures**, requiring extensive human intervention for updates and improvements. However, with advancements in **machine learning (ML), deep learning (DL), and large language models (LLMs)**, AI workflows have evolved into **modular, automated, and continuously improving systems**.

Traditional AI pipelines followed a **linear, sequential** execution model. However, modern AI workflows leverage **graph-based execution models**, where AI agents, decision nodes, and feedback loops create **adaptive, stateful, and intelligent automation**.

For example, an **AI-powered document processing system** doesn't just extract text and classify it—it continuously **improves its accuracy by learning from user feedback** and dynamically adjusting its processing logic.

Key Components of an AI Workflow

A complete AI workflow consists of multiple interconnected components, each playing a vital role in transforming raw data into intelligent actions.

1. Data Collection & Ingestion

AI workflows begin with **gathering and integrating data** from various sources, including databases, APIs, IoT devices, and real-time streams. This stage is critical as AI models rely on **high-quality, diverse, and well-structured data** to make accurate predictions.

Example sources:

- **Structured data:** SQL databases, CSV files
- **Unstructured data:** Text, images, audio, video
- **Streaming data:** Logs, telemetry, social media feeds

LangGraph and LangChain in Data Collection

With **LangChain**, AI workflows can efficiently **fetch and process data from APIs, vector databases, and document stores**, making it an ideal tool for intelligent knowledge retrieval. **LangGraph**, in turn, structures how these retrieval processes interact within an automated AI pipeline.

---

2. Data Preprocessing & Feature Engineering

Raw data is often **messy, inconsistent, or incomplete**, requiring cleaning and transformation before being fed into AI models. This step includes:

- **Handling missing values** (imputing, removing)
- **Normalizing and scaling** numerical data
- **Tokenizing and vectorizing** text for NLP models
- **Extracting relevant features** to improve model performance

Code Example: Preprocessing Text for AI Workflows

Python (LangChain + NLP Preprocessing)

python

```
from langchain.text_splitter import RecursiveCharacterTextSplitter

# Sample text

text = "AI workflows automate machine learning tasks. They improve efficiency and scalability."



# Splitting text into chunks for better processing

text_splitter = RecursiveCharacterTextSplitter(chunk_size=50, chunk_overlap=5)
```

```
chunks = text_splitter.split_text(text)


print(chunks)
```

Explanation:

- The **text is split into smaller, manageable chunks**.
- This is useful for **retrieval-augmented generation (RAG)** when working with **LLMs and vector databases**.

---

3. Model Training & Fine-Tuning

Once the data is ready, AI models are trained to recognize patterns, make predictions, or generate outputs. This stage involves:

- **Choosing an appropriate model architecture** (ML, DL, or LLMs)
- **Training models on labeled data**
- **Fine-tuning pre-trained models** for domain-specific tasks

Example: Fine-Tuning an LLM with LangChain

Fine-tuning **enhances model accuracy for specific tasks,** such as domain-specific chatbots or industry-specific AI assistants.

```python
from langchain.llms import OpenAI

# Load a pre-trained model and fine-tune it

llm = OpenAI(model_name="gpt-4")


response = llm.predict("Summarize AI workflows in 50 words.")

print(response)
```

Explanation:

- The **pre-trained LLM is used to summarize AI workflows**.
- Fine-tuning can further **adapt models to specific business use cases**.

---

4. Inference & Real-Time Predictions

Inference is where AI models generate predictions based on new data. **Optimized, low-latency inference** is crucial for real-time applications such as:

- **Chatbots and AI assistants**

- **Fraud detection systems**
- **AI-powered search engines**

LangGraph's Role in Real-Time Inference

LangGraph enhances inference workflows by **managing stateful interactions** between different AI components. Unlike traditional ML pipelines that output **a single prediction, LangGraph-based AI systems interact dynamically with users**, refining responses based on **previous interactions and external data sources**.

---

5. Decision Logic & AI Agents

Beyond inference, AI workflows often involve **decision-making**, where **multiple AI agents collaborate** to determine the best course of action. This is especially useful in:

- **Autonomous customer support**
- **AI-driven content generation**
- **Adaptive recommendation engines**

Example: Multi-Agent AI Workflow in LangGraph

LangGraph enables **multi-agent decision workflows**, where different AI components handle **retrieval, reasoning, and response generation**.

python

```python
from langgraph.graph import Graph

# Create an AI Workflow Graph

workflow = Graph()


# Define nodes (AI agents)

workflow.add_node("query", function=query_user)

workflow.add_node("retrieve", function=retrieve_knowledge)

workflow.add_node("respond", function=generate_response)


# Define edges (workflow logic)

workflow.add_edge("query", "retrieve")

workflow.add_edge("retrieve", "respond")


# Execute the workflow

workflow.run("What is an AI workflow?")
```

Explanation:

- This AI workflow dynamically **retrieves relevant knowledge** and **generates context-aware responses**.
- Unlike traditional rule-based systems, **LangGraph-powered workflows adapt and improve over time**.

---

6. Monitoring & Optimization

AI workflows **require continuous monitoring** to maintain accuracy, reliability, and efficiency. **Key considerations include:**

- **Detecting data drift** – Ensuring that model predictions remain accurate as data changes.
- **Performance tuning** – Optimizing inference latency and computational efficiency.
- **Logging & Observability** – Tracking model behavior using tools like **LangSmith** for debugging.

Example: AI Workflow Monitoring with LangSmith

python

```python
from langsmith import LangSmith

# Initialize LangSmith monitoring

monitor = LangSmith(project="AI Workflow Monitoring")
```

```
# Log AI predictions

monitor.log_event("Prediction", data={"query": "What is AI?",
"response": "AI is..."} )
```

Explanation:

- **Tracks AI interactions and performance over time.**
- **Helps identify failures or biases in AI models.**

1.2 Why LangGraph and LangChain?

Introduction

In the rapidly evolving AI landscape, **orchestrating complex workflows efficiently** is a significant challenge. Traditional AI pipelines often struggle with **scalability, adaptability, and seamless multi-agent collaboration**, making it difficult to build **modular, maintainable, and intelligent automation systems**.

This is where **LangGraph and LangChain** excel. These tools provide **a powerful framework for designing and executing AI-driven workflows** that can dynamically adapt, incorporate external knowledge sources, and **enhance AI decision-making through stateful graph-based execution**.

This chapter explores:

- **The limitations of traditional AI pipelines**
- **How LangGraph and LangChain solve these challenges**
- **Real-world use cases where LangGraph and LangChain provide significant advantages**
- **Practical examples of implementing AI workflows using these tools**

The Limitations of Traditional AI Pipelines

Before delving into why LangGraph and LangChain stand out, it's important to understand the constraints of conventional AI pipelines.

1. Linear, Sequential Execution

Traditional AI workflows operate in a **strict, step-by-step manner**, where each stage depends entirely on the previous one. This makes it difficult to introduce **parallel processing, dynamic decision-making, or adaptive learning**.

Example problem:

- A **customer support chatbot** using a traditional pipeline follows predefined **if-else logic**, making it **rigid and unable to handle evolving conversations dynamically**.

2. Stateless Interactions

Most traditional AI pipelines **do not retain memory of past interactions**. This creates problems in scenarios requiring **context retention, adaptive behavior, and long-term reasoning**.

Example problem:

- A **legal document assistant** might analyze contracts but **fail to remember prior sections**, leading to inconsistencies in contract summaries.

3. Lack of Multi-Agent Collaboration

AI applications often require **multiple specialized agents**—for retrieval, summarization, translation, reasoning, and response generation. Traditional workflows struggle to coordinate **multiple AI components dynamically**.

Example problem:

- A **news summarization AI** may require **fact-checking from a retrieval agent, sentiment analysis from another model**, and **text simplification from yet another module**. Coordinating these modules **efficiently in a traditional pipeline is difficult**.

4. Difficulty in Scaling and Modularity

Most AI pipelines are **hardcoded**, making it difficult to add **new functionalities** or **scale components** independently. **Graph-based AI execution, like LangGraph, solves this by enabling modular, flexible AI architectures.**

Why LangGraph and LangChain?

LangGraph and LangChain solve these limitations by introducing:

- **Graph-based, non-linear execution**
- **Stateful interactions with persistent memory**
- **Multi-agent collaboration and decision-making**
- **Seamless integration with external knowledge sources**

1. LangChain: A Modular AI Framework

LangChain provides a **powerful abstraction layer for integrating LLMs, vector databases, APIs, and external data sources.**

Key Features:

- **Seamless AI workflow orchestration**
- **Retrieval-augmented generation (RAG) capabilities**
- **Pre-built integrations with vector databases, APIs, and custom tools**

Example: Using LangChain for Knowledge Retrieval

Python (LangChain)

python

```python
from langchain.chains import RetrievalQA

from langchain.vectorstores import FAISS

from langchain.embeddings.openai import OpenAIEmbeddings

from langchain.llms import OpenAI


# Initialize a vector database for document retrieval
vector_store = FAISS.load_local("my_document_store", OpenAIEmbeddings())


# Create a retrieval-based QA pipeline
qa = RetrievalQA.from_chain_type(llm=OpenAI(mod
```

```
el_name="gpt-4"),
retriever=vector_store.as_retriever())

# Ask a question based on stored knowledge

response = qa.run("What are AI workflows?")

print(response)
```

Explanation:

- **Uses LangChain to fetch relevant knowledge** from a vector database.
- **Enhances AI responses with external data**, making LLMs more context-aware.

---

2. LangGraph: Enabling Graph-Based AI Execution

LangGraph extends LangChain by providing **graph-based execution, enabling dynamic AI workflows with multiple interacting agents**.

Key Features:

- **Non-linear, graph-based workflows**
- **Stateful memory, enabling long-term AI reasoning**

- **Multi-agent AI collaboration with decision-making logic**

Building an AI Workflow with LangGraph

Let's walk through a **real-world AI workflow** using LangGraph:

Use Case: AI-Powered Legal Document Review
An AI system that:

1. **Retrieves case law references**
2. **Summarizes key legal points**
3. **Checks document consistency**
4. **Generates a final report**

Step 1: Setting Up a LangGraph Workflow

python

```python
from langgraph.graph import Graph

# Define the AI workflow as a graph

workflow = Graph()


# Add workflow components (agents)
```

```
workflow.add_node("retrieve_case_laws",
function=retrieve_legal_cases)

workflow.add_node("summarize_key_points",
function=summarize_text)

workflow.add_node("check_consistency",
function=check_document_coherence)

workflow.add_node("generate_report",
function=generate_final_summary)


# Define workflow execution flow

workflow.add_edge("retrieve_case_laws",
"summarize_key_points")

workflow.add_edge("summarize_key_points",
"check_consistency")

workflow.add_edge("check_consistency",
"generate_report")


# Run the AI workflow

workflow.run("Analyze this legal document
for key case laws.")
```

Step 2: Implementing Workflow Nodes (Agents)

Retrieving Case Laws

python

```python
def retrieve_legal_cases(document_text):

    """Fetches relevant legal cases using a
vector database."""

    return
vector_store.search(document_text,
top_k=5)
```

Summarizing Key Legal Points

python

```python
def summarize_text(case_laws):

    """Summarizes   key   legal   references
using an LLM."""

    return   llm.predict(f"Summarize   these
case laws: {case_laws}")
```

Checking Document Consistency

python

```python
def check_document_coherence(summary):

    """Verifies if the summary is
consistent and logical."""

    return            llm.predict(f"Verify
consistency   of   this   legal   summary:
{summary}")
```

Generating Final Report

python

```python
def
generate_final_summary(verified_summary):

    """Creates a structured legal document
summary report."""

    return            f"Final           Report:
{verified_summary}"
```

Why This Approach Works

Feature	Traditional AI Pipeline	LangGraph + LangChain
Workflow Execution	Linear, rigid steps	Flexible, graph-based execution
State Management	Stateless processing	Persistent memory for context-aware AI
Multi-Agent Support	Hard to coordinate agents	Seamless multi-agent workflows
Scalability	Difficult to extend	Modular and highly scalable

Real-World Use Cases

LangGraph and LangChain are **widely used in industry** for:

- **AI-powered legal research** (Summarizing case laws)
- **Automated customer support** (Multi-agent AI chatbots)
- **Financial fraud detection** (Graph-based decision-making)
- **Content generation pipelines** (Coordinating LLMs, retrieval, and filtering)

1.3 Real-World Applications

AI-powered workflows have revolutionized industries by enabling **automated decision-making, knowledge retrieval, natural language processing, and multi-agent collaboration**. While many AI solutions focus on isolated tasks—such as answering questions or generating content—LangGraph and LangChain enable the **orchestration of complex, scalable, and intelligent workflows** that interact with real-world data, perform reasoning, and integrate multiple AI agents.

In this chapter, we explore **practical, real-world applications** powered by LangGraph and LangChain, providing:

- **Detailed explanations of industry use cases**
- **Hands-on implementation examples with complete code**
- **Best practices, optimizations, and troubleshooting strategies**

By the end of this chapter, you will have **a clear understanding of how to build and scale AI applications using graph-based workflow automation**.

---

1. AI-Powered Customer Support Assistants

Use Case Overview

Many businesses rely on **AI-driven customer support agents** to handle user inquiries, automate troubleshooting, and provide **seamless, context-aware conversations**.

Traditional chatbots often follow **rigid rule-based logic**, but **LangGraph enables multi-agent reasoning**, where:

1. **An intent classifier** determines the customer's request.
2. **A retrieval-based agent** fetches relevant knowledge.
3. **A reasoning agent** generates a response.
4. **An escalation handler** routes unresolved queries to a human agent.

Building a Customer Support AI Workflow

Step 1: Define Workflow Nodes

Python (LangGraph-based AI Chatbot)

python

```python
from langgraph.graph import Graph
from langchain.llms import OpenAI
from langchain.vectorstores import FAISS

# Initialize LLM and vector database
llm = OpenAI(model_name="gpt-4")
vector_store                           =
FAISS.load_local("support_docs",
OpenAIEmbeddings())

# Define AI agents
def classify_intent(user_query):
    """Identifies    user    intent    from
query."""
    return    llm.predict(f"Classify    the
intent of this query: {user_query}")

def retrieve_knowledge(user_query):
    """Fetches    relevant    knowledge    from
stored documents."""
    return vector_store.search(user_query,
top_k=3)

def generate_response(knowledge):
    """Generates   a   response   based   on
retrieved knowledge."""
```

```python
    return    llm.predict(f"Generate    a
customer-friendly response: {knowledge}")

def escalate_to_human(user_query):
    """Routes unresolved queries to human
support."""
    return "Escalating to human support..."

# Create workflow graph
workflow = Graph()
workflow.add_node("classify_intent",
classify_intent)
workflow.add_node("retrieve_knowledge",
retrieve_knowledge)
workflow.add_node("generate_response",
generate_response)
workflow.add_node("escalate_to_human",
escalate_to_human)

# Define execution paths
workflow.add_edge("classify_intent",
"retrieve_knowledge",      condition=lambda
intent: intent != "human_escalation")
workflow.add_edge("retrieve_knowledge",
"generate_response")
```

```
workflow.add_edge("classify_intent",
"escalate_to_human",        condition=lambda
intent: intent == "human_escalation")

# Execute chatbot workflow
response = workflow.run("How can I reset my
password?")
print(response)
```

Why This Works

- **Dynamic multi-agent coordination** enables adaptive responses.
- **Graph-based execution** allows **parallel and conditional decision-making**.
- **Memory persistence** ensures context-aware interactions.

Real-World Impact:

- Reduces **customer support costs** by up to 70%.
- Provides **instant responses** and improves customer satisfaction.

---

2. AI-Powered Legal Document Analysis

Use Case Overview

Law firms and legal professionals spend countless hours **analyzing contracts, extracting key clauses, and verifying compliance**. AI can automate this process by:

1. **Extracting relevant clauses** using retrieval-based AI.
2. **Summarizing legal points** with an LLM.
3. **Checking for inconsistencies** in contract wording.
4. **Providing a risk assessment** for legal teams.

Implementing AI for Legal Document Analysis

python

```python
def extract_clauses(document_text):
    """Retrieves key contract clauses."""
    return
vector_store.search(document_text,
top_k=5)


def summarize_legal_points(clauses):
    """Summarizes      the      extracted
clauses."""
    return    llm.predict(f"Summarize   the
following legal clauses: {clauses}")


def check_contract_consistency(summary):
```

```python
    """Verifies legal consistency of
contract wording."""
    return     llm.predict(f"Check    for
inconsistencies in this legal summary:
{summary}")

def
generate_risk_assessment(verified_summary)
:
    """Provides    a    risk    assessment
report."""
    return    f"Risk    Analysis    Report:
{verified_summary}"
```

Workflow Execution

python

```python
workflow = Graph()
workflow.add_node("extract_clauses",
extract_clauses)
workflow.add_node("summarize_legal_points"
, summarize_legal_points)
workflow.add_node("check_contract_consiste
ncy", check_contract_consistency)
```

```
workflow.add_node("generate_risk_assessmen
t", generate_risk_assessment)

workflow.add_edge("extract_clauses",
"summarize_legal_points")
workflow.add_edge("summarize_legal_points"
, "check_contract_consistency")
workflow.add_edge("check_contract_consiste
ncy", "generate_risk_assessment")

# Run the workflow
report   =   workflow.run("Analyze    this
contract for compliance.")
print(report)
```

Real-World Impact:

- Automates **contract review** for law firms.
- Reduces **legal risk** by detecting inconsistencies.
- Saves **hours of manual legal work** per case.

---

3. AI-Driven Financial Fraud Detection

Use Case Overview

Banks and financial institutions must **identify fraudulent transactions in real-time** to prevent financial losses. A graph-based AI system can:

1. **Analyze user transaction patterns** for anomalies.
2. **Score transactions based on risk factors.**
3. **Trigger alerts for suspicious activity.**

Building a Fraud Detection Pipeline

python

```python
def analyze_transaction(transaction):
    """Detects anomalies in a financial transaction."""
    return llm.predict(f"Analyze the following transaction for fraud risk: {transaction}")


def score_risk(transaction_analysis):
    """Assigns a fraud risk score."""
    return llm.predict(f"Assign a fraud risk score based on analysis: {transaction_analysis}")


def trigger_alert(risk_score):
```

```python
    """Triggers an alert if the risk score
is high."""
    return "Alert triggered!" if risk_score
> 80 else "No fraud detected."
```

Workflow Execution:

python

```python
workflow = Graph()
workflow.add_node("analyze_transaction",
analyze_transaction)
workflow.add_node("score_risk",
score_risk)
workflow.add_node("trigger_alert",
trigger_alert)

workflow.add_edge("analyze_transaction",
"score_risk")
workflow.add_edge("score_risk",
"trigger_alert")

result    =    workflow.run("Transaction:
$10,000 wire transfer to unknown account.")
print(result)
```

Why This Works

- Uses **graph-based decision-making** for fraud risk assessment.
- **Integrates LLM-based anomaly detection** for better accuracy.
- **Reduces false positives** compared to rule-based fraud detection.

Real-World Impact:

- Helps banks **prevent fraud in real-time**.
- Reduces **financial losses** and compliance risks.

Chapter 2: Understanding LangGraph and LangChain

The development of AI applications often involves managing **complex workflows, orchestrating multiple agents, integrating external data sources, and ensuring efficient execution**. Traditional approaches to AI pipeline design often rely on **linear, rule-based systems** that struggle with adaptability, state management, and parallel execution.

LangGraph and LangChain provide a **powerful framework for building graph-based AI workflows**, allowing developers to create **scalable, modular, and highly interactive AI systems**. In this chapter, we will:

- **Explore the core principles of LangGraph and LangChain.**
- **Understand their key features and advantages in AI workflow development.**
- **Walk through the installation and setup process to get started.**

By the end of this chapter, you will have a **strong foundational understanding** of how these tools work and how they fit into modern AI development.

2.1 Overview of LangGraph and LangChain

AI-powered applications are becoming increasingly complex, requiring robust frameworks to manage workflows, dependencies, and interactions efficiently. LangGraph and LangChain are two powerful tools that enable developers to design, orchestrate, and scale AI-driven workflows with modular, reusable components. This section provides a deep dive into these frameworks, explaining their core capabilities and how they complement each other in building sophisticated AI pipelines.

What is LangGraph?

LangGraph is a framework designed to facilitate the construction of AI workflows using graph-based execution models. Unlike traditional linear workflows, LangGraph allows for flexible, non-linear execution paths, making it well-suited for complex AI applications involving decision trees, conditional logic, and multi-agent collaboration.

Key Characteristics of LangGraph:

1. **Graph-Based Execution** – Workflows are structured as directed graphs, where nodes represent individual tasks and edges define dependencies and execution paths.

2. **Parallel Processing** – LangGraph supports concurrent task execution, optimizing performance for large-scale AI workflows.

3. **State Management** – The framework provides built-in mechanisms for maintaining and tracking state across workflow executions.

4. **Modular and Composable** – Tasks and workflows can be modularized, enabling reuse across different applications.

Use Cases of LangGraph:

- **Multi-Agent AI Systems** – Coordinating interactions between different AI agents handling distinct tasks.
- **Decision Tree-Based AI** – Implementing conditional AI workflows that dynamically adapt based on input.
- **Automated Data Processing Pipelines** – Handling complex ETL (Extract, Transform, Load) operations in AI-driven data workflows.

What is LangChain?

LangChain is a widely adopted framework that simplifies the integration of language models into applications. It provides a structured approach for building AI-powered systems, offering tools for data retrieval, prompt engineering, memory handling, and interaction chaining.

Key Characteristics of LangChain:

1. **Modular Architecture** – LangChain is built on a component-based structure, allowing developers to integrate only the necessary modules for their specific needs.

2. **Memory and Context Management** – The framework supports short-term and long-term memory handling, enabling AI models to maintain state across interactions.

3. **Integration with External Tools** – LangChain provides seamless connectivity to databases, APIs, and third-party services.

4. **Support for Agents and Chains** – Developers can define complex reasoning patterns, chaining multiple AI models and functions together in a structured workflow.

Use Cases of LangChain:

- **Conversational AI** – Building chatbots and virtual assistants with persistent memory.

- **Retrieval-Augmented Generation (RAG)** – Enhancing AI responses by integrating external knowledge bases.

- **Automated Report Generation** – Streamlining document creation using AI-driven templates and structured content generation.

How LangGraph and LangChain Work Together

While LangChain provides a solid foundation for handling AI model interactions, LangGraph extends its capabilities by introducing advanced workflow orchestration. The combination of these two frameworks allows developers to create AI applications that are:

1. **Scalable** – AI workflows can handle high-throughput demands efficiently.
2. **Adaptive** – Systems can make real-time decisions based on dynamic conditions.
3. **Composable** – Components can be reused across different AI applications, reducing development time.

For example, an AI-powered customer support system might use LangChain for natural language understanding while leveraging LangGraph to manage conversation flow, escalate issues, and trigger automated actions.

2.2 Key Features and Benefits

LangGraph and LangChain provide a powerful foundation for building AI-driven applications by enabling structured workflow execution, efficient orchestration, and modular AI interactions. This section explores their core features, illustrating how they enhance AI development, streamline automation, and enable the creation of scalable and adaptive systems.

Key Features of LangGraph

1. Graph-Based Execution Model

LangGraph structures workflows as directed graphs, where nodes represent tasks and edges define dependencies. This enables complex, non-linear execution paths, making it ideal for dynamic AI applications.

Example Use Case:

- A **multi-step document processing pipeline** where AI components handle OCR, entity recognition, summarization, and content validation in parallel.

Key Benefits:

- Enables complex decision-making with branching logic.
- Supports dynamic execution paths that adapt to real-time data.
- Improves efficiency by allowing multiple tasks to run concurrently.

---

2. Parallel and Asynchronous Processing

LangGraph allows tasks to be executed in parallel, reducing latency in AI workflows.

Example Use Case:

- A **real-time customer support AI** where different agents handle inquiries, escalation, and resolution simultaneously.

Key Benefits:

- Improves processing speed for large-scale applications.
- Supports multi-agent collaboration within AI workflows.
- Reduces bottlenecks by executing independent tasks in parallel.

---

3. Stateful Workflow Management

LangGraph maintains workflow state across execution cycles, ensuring seamless tracking and decision-making.

Example Use Case:

- A **fraud detection system** that analyzes multiple financial transactions over time, storing intermediate results for further evaluation.

Key Benefits:

- Ensures AI models retain relevant historical context.
- Enables long-running workflows with persistence.
- Facilitates debugging and monitoring of AI-driven processes.

4. Modularity and Reusability

LangGraph promotes code reuse by allowing developers to define reusable workflow components.

Example Use Case:

- A **voice assistant** where modular AI tasks handle voice recognition, intent detection, and response generation separately.

Key Benefits:

- Reduces redundancy by leveraging predefined workflow components.
- Encourages maintainable and extensible AI system design.
- Allows rapid prototyping of new AI capabilities.

Key Features of LangChain

1. Modular Components for AI Integration

LangChain provides pre-built components for connecting AI models with external data sources, APIs, and tools.

Example Use Case:

- A **retrieval-augmented generation (RAG) system** that fetches relevant data from a knowledge base before generating a response.

Key Benefits:

- Simplifies the integration of AI models with real-world applications.
- Enhances AI responses by incorporating structured data sources.
- Reduces the complexity of building knowledge-driven AI systems.

2. Memory and Context Handling

LangChain supports both short-term and long-term memory management, allowing AI models to maintain context across interactions.

Example Use Case:

- A **legal AI assistant** that remembers case details from previous conversations and provides consistent advice.

Key Benefits:

- Improves user experience by maintaining session continuity.
- Enables more intelligent and context-aware AI applications.
- Supports adaptive learning models that refine responses over time.

---

3. Seamless Agent and Tool Integration

LangChain allows AI models to interact with external tools, APIs, and databases.

Example Use Case:

- A **financial chatbot** that pulls live stock data, analyzes trends, and provides investment insights.

Key Benefits:

- Expands AI capabilities beyond simple text-based interactions.
- Enables intelligent automation with real-time data access.
- Supports multi-agent architectures where AI models collaborate on complex tasks.

4. Chainable AI Workflows

LangChain allows AI workflows to be structured as sequences of interdependent processing steps.

Example Use Case:

- A **medical diagnosis AI** that sequentially analyzes symptoms, matches patterns, and provides recommendations.

Key Benefits:

- Supports structured, multi-step reasoning for AI applications.
- Enhances explainability by breaking down AI decision-making into clear steps.
- Allows greater control over AI-driven decision logic.

How LangGraph and LangChain Complement Each Other

While LangChain specializes in model interactions, LangGraph enhances AI workflows by structuring execution paths and state management. Their combined use unlocks powerful capabilities:

Feature	LangGraph	LangChain	Combined Benefit
Execution Model	Graph-based workflows	Chain-based model execution	Structured AI pipelines
Concurrency	Parallel task execution	Sequential model calls	Optimized processing
Memory Management	Workflow state tracking	AI context memory	Long-term and session memory
Tool Integration	Task orchestration	API and tool connections	Intelligent automation
Scalability	Distributed workflow execution	Modular AI model handling	Production-ready AI applications

Example Use Case:

- A **legal document review AI** that:
    1. Uses LangChain to extract relevant case law from multiple sources.
    2. Employs LangGraph to orchestrate various review stages (text parsing, legal interpretation, summarization).
    3. Integrates LangChain again to refine the results with a language model before final output.

This approach ensures efficient document processing with structured execution and intelligent reasoning.

2.3 Installation and Setup

Before diving into building AI-driven workflows with LangGraph and LangChain, it is essential to set up a proper development environment. This section provides a step-by-step guide to installing and configuring both libraries, ensuring that your system is prepared for hands-on development. It covers installation for different operating systems, dependencies, and verification steps to confirm a successful setup.

1. Setting Up the Development Environment

1.1 Prerequisites

Before installing LangGraph and LangChain, ensure that your system meets the following requirements:

System Requirements

- **Operating System:** Windows, macOS, or Linux
- **Python Version:** 3.8 or later
- **Package Manager:** `pip` (Python's package manager)
- **Virtual Environment (Recommended):** `venv` or `conda`

Dependencies

Both LangGraph and LangChain rely on external libraries such as `networkx` for graph-based workflows and `openai` for AI model interactions. These will be installed automatically when setting up the libraries.

1.2 Creating a Virtual Environment

It is best practice to create a virtual environment to isolate dependencies and prevent conflicts with system-wide packages.

Using `venv` (Recommended for Most Users)

Run the following commands in your terminal or command prompt:

sh

```
# Create a new virtual environment

python -m venv langgraph_env

# Activate the virtual environment

# On Windows:

langgraph_env\Scripts\activate

# On macOS/Linux:

source langgraph_env/bin/activate
```

Using conda (Alternative for Anaconda Users)

sh

```
# Create a new conda environment

conda create --name langgraph_env python=3.10

# Activate the environment

conda activate langgraph_env
```

Once activated, all installations will be confined to this environment.

---

2. Installing LangGraph and LangChain

2.1 Installing LangGraph

LangGraph can be installed directly from PyPI using `pip`:

sh

```
pip install langgraph
```

This command installs LangGraph along with its dependencies, including `networkx` for handling graph-based workflows.

To verify the installation, run the following command:

python

```
python -c "import langgraph; print(langgraph.__version__)"
```

If the installation is successful, it will output the installed version of LangGraph.

2.2 Installing LangChain

LangChain is also available via PyPI and can be installed with:

sh

```
pip install langchain
```

To verify the installation, run:

python

```
python -c "import langchain;
print(langchain.__version__)"
```

2.3 Installing Additional Dependencies

Depending on the AI models and integrations you plan to use, you may need to install additional libraries. Common dependencies include:

sh

```
pip install openai langchain-openai

pip install tiktoken  # Tokenization
library for handling text chunks

pip install pydantic  # Data validation and
settings management

pip install networkx  # Graph-based
processing support
```

For interacting with local models, consider:

sh

```
pip install transformers sentence-
transformers
```

3. Verifying the Installation

3.1 Running a Basic LangGraph Workflow

To confirm that LangGraph is installed correctly, run the following script, which defines a simple workflow with two nodes:

Python

python

```python
import langgraph

# Create a new graph

graph = langgraph.Graph()

# Define a simple function as a node

def greet():
    return "Hello, LangGraph!"


# Add the function to the graph

graph.add_node("greeting", greet)


# Execute the graph

result = graph.run()

print(result)
```

If the setup is correct, the output should display `"Hello, LangGraph!"`.

3.2 Running a Basic LangChain Pipeline

To verify LangChain, create a simple text processing chain:

Python

python

```python
from langchain.llms import OpenAI

from langchain.chains import LLMChain

from          langchain.prompts          import
PromptTemplate


# Define a prompt template

prompt = PromptTemplate(

    input_variables=["question"],

    template="What   is   the   capital   of
{question}?"

)
```

```python
# Create a chain

llm = OpenAI(model="gpt-3.5-turbo")    # Ensure you have API access

chain = LLMChain(llm=llm, prompt=prompt)


# Run the chain

response = chain.run("France")

print(response)
```

Note: Replace `gpt-3.5-turbo` with the model available in your OpenAI account.

---

4. Common Installation Issues and Troubleshooting

4.1 Dependency Conflicts

If you encounter dependency conflicts during installation, use the `--upgrade` flag:

sh

```
pip install --upgrade langgraph langchain
```

For a clean installation, try:

sh

```
pip uninstall langgraph langchain -y
pip install langgraph langchain
```

4.2 OpenAI API Key Issues

If using OpenAI models, ensure you have set up your API key:

sh

```
export OPENAI_API_KEY="your-api-key"   # macOS/Linux
set  OPENAI_API_KEY="your-api-key"   # Windows
```

Or, set it within your Python script:

Python

python

```
import os

os.environ["OPENAI_API_KEY"] = "your-api-
key"
```

4.3 Virtual Environment Not Activating

If the virtual environment does not activate, ensure that:

- On Windows, you are using **Command Prompt** (not PowerShell).
- On macOS/Linux, you have permission to execute scripts (`chmod +x` if necessary).

Chapter 3: Fundamentals of Graph-Based AI Pipelines

As AI workflows become increasingly complex, traditional linear pipelines often struggle with efficiency, scalability, and flexibility. Graph-based AI pipelines address these challenges by modeling workflows as directed graphs, where tasks (nodes) are connected by dependencies (edges). This approach allows for parallel execution, dynamic adaptability, and better resource optimization.

This chapter explores the core concepts of graph-based AI pipelines, breaking them down into three key sections:

- **3.1 What are Graph-Based AI Pipelines?** – Understanding the fundamental structure and advantages of graph-based pipelines.
- **3.2 Understanding Nodes, Edges, and Dependencies** – A deep dive into the components that define graph-based workflows.
- **3.3 Designing Scalable AI Workflows** – Best practices for building robust and scalable AI pipelines using graph structures.

By the end of this chapter, you will have a strong foundation in graph-based AI workflows and be prepared to build complex, scalable AI automation systems with LangGraph and LangChain.

3.1 What are Graph-Based AI Pipelines?

AI pipelines are essential for automating machine learning workflows, enabling data ingestion, processing, model inference, and decision-making. Traditionally, AI pipelines follow a linear structure, where each stage depends strictly on the previous one. However, as AI applications become more complex, the need for more **flexible, scalable, and efficient** execution models has emerged.

Graph-based AI pipelines address these challenges by **modeling AI workflows as directed graphs** rather than fixed sequences. In these pipelines, tasks (represented as **nodes**) are connected by dependencies (**edges**), allowing multiple tasks to execute concurrently, dynamically adapt to conditions, and optimize resource allocation.

This section explores the **fundamentals of graph-based AI pipelines**, their **advantages over traditional pipelines**, and **real-world use cases**.

Understanding AI Pipelines

What is an AI Pipeline?

An AI pipeline is a structured process that automates the flow of data through different AI tasks, ensuring that models receive the right inputs and generate useful outputs. These tasks can include:

- **Data ingestion** (extracting raw data from sources)
- **Preprocessing** (cleaning, transforming, and normalizing data)
- **Feature engineering** (extracting relevant features for ML models)
- **Model inference** (applying trained models to make predictions)
- **Post-processing** (refining outputs and formatting results)
- **Decision-making** (integrating predictions into applications)

Limitations of Traditional (Linear) Pipelines

Traditional AI pipelines typically follow a **linear execution model**, where each step strictly follows another in sequence. While this structure works well for simple workflows, it becomes problematic for **large-scale, dynamic, and multi-task AI applications** due to:

1. **Limited Scalability:** Linear pipelines often create bottlenecks as all tasks must execute sequentially, preventing efficient resource utilization.
2. **Poor Adaptability:** Conditional logic and dynamic execution paths are difficult to implement in static pipelines.
3. **Redundant Computation:** If multiple processes require the same intermediate results, they may have to recompute them separately.
4. **Inefficient Error Handling:** Failures in one step may break the entire pipeline, making fault tolerance challenging.

To overcome these challenges, **graph-based AI pipelines** provide a more efficient and flexible approach.

Graph-Based AI Pipelines: A Paradigm Shift

What is a Graph-Based AI Pipeline?

A **graph-based AI pipeline** structures tasks and dependencies as a **Directed Acyclic Graph (DAG)**, where:

- **Nodes** represent tasks (e.g., data processing, inference, decision-making).
- **Edges** define dependencies between tasks, determining execution order.

Unlike linear pipelines, graph-based pipelines allow:

- **Parallel execution** of independent tasks.
- **Dynamic branching** based on conditions.
- **Reusability** of common processing steps across workflows.
- **Scalability** by efficiently managing complex dependencies.

Key Characteristics of Graph-Based Pipelines

Feature	Graph-Based Pipelines	Traditional Pipelines
Execution Flow	Dynamic & Parallel	Fixed & Sequential
Scalability	High (handles large workflows)	Limited (single execution path)
Adaptability	Supports conditional execution	Requires hard-coded logic
Fault Tolerance	Can rerun specific nodes upon failure	Entire pipeline may fail

Resource Utilization	Optimized (parallel execution)	Less efficient

Real-World Applications of Graph-Based AI Pipelines

Graph-based pipelines are widely used in **machine learning, natural language processing (NLP), and AI-driven automation**. Some common applications include:

1. Machine Learning (ML) Model Training Pipelines

Scenario: A company trains a machine learning model for fraud detection. The pipeline involves:

- **Data Preprocessing** (cleaning transaction logs).
- **Feature Engineering** (extracting behavioral patterns).
- **Model Training** (training classifiers in parallel with different hyperparameters).
- **Model Evaluation** (comparing models and selecting the best one).

Graph-based solution: Parallel training of multiple models can occur simultaneously, optimizing hyperparameter selection efficiently.

2. NLP Pipelines for AI Assistants

Scenario: A virtual assistant processes user input, responding with personalized answers. The workflow includes:

- **Speech-to-Text (STT)** (converting spoken words into text).
- **Named Entity Recognition (NER)** (identifying key entities in the text).
- **Sentiment Analysis** (detecting user sentiment).
- **Response Generation** (generating answers based on detected intent).

Graph-based solution: The **NER and sentiment analysis** steps can run **in parallel**, reducing response time.

3. AI-Powered Document Processing

Scenario: A legal document processing system extracts key details and summarizes information. The pipeline includes:

- **Text Extraction** (extracting text from scanned PDFs).
- **Summarization** (generating concise summaries).
- **Translation** (translating summaries into multiple languages).
- **Sentiment Analysis** (classifying the document's tone).

Graph-based solution: The summarization and translation steps can run concurrently, increasing efficiency.

Implementing a Simple Graph-Based AI Pipeline with LangGraph

1. Defining the Workflow

The following example demonstrates a **text processing AI pipeline** using LangGraph. This pipeline:

- Extracts text from input.
- Summarizes the content.
- Translates the summary into another language.

Python

python

```python
import langgraph

# Define nodes (tasks)

def extract_text(data):

    return                              {"text":
data["document"].split()}   # Tokenizing
words
```

```python
def summarize_text(data):

    return             {"summary":            "
".join(data["text"][:10])}    #  Summarize
first 10 words

def translate_text(data):

    return {"translated": "Traducción: " +
data["summary"]}  # Spanish translation


# Create a graph

graph = langgraph.Graph()


# Add nodes to the graph

graph.add_node("extract_text",
extract_text)

graph.add_node("summarize_text",
summarize_text)

graph.add_node("translate_text",
translate_text)
```

```
# Define execution order

graph.add_edge("extract_text",
"summarize_text")

graph.add_edge("summarize_text",
"translate_text")


# Run the pipeline

input_data = {"document": "Graph-based AI
pipelines enable efficient execution of
complex workflows."}

result = graph.run(input_data)

print(result)
```

2. Understanding the Execution Flow

1. The **extract_text** node tokenizes the document.
2. The **summarize_text** node generates a summary.
3. The **translate_text** node translates the summary into Spanish.

This modular approach enables efficient processing with **clear task dependencies**.

3.2 Understanding Nodes, Edges, and Dependencies

Graph-based AI pipelines rely on three core components: **nodes, edges, and dependencies**. These elements define how tasks are structured, executed, and interconnected in an AI workflow. Unlike traditional linear pipelines, which follow a strict sequential order, **graph-based workflows allow for dynamic, parallel, and scalable execution**.

This chapter provides an in-depth understanding of **nodes, edges, and dependencies**, explaining their role in **building flexible and efficient AI pipelines**. We will cover their **technical details, real-world applications, and practical implementations** using LangGraph.

---

1. Nodes: The Building Blocks of AI Pipelines

What is a Node?

A **node** in a graph-based AI pipeline represents a **computational unit**—a discrete task that processes data and produces an output.

Each node is **self-contained**, meaning it performs a specific operation independently, whether it be:

- **Data preprocessing** (e.g., tokenizing text, normalizing images).
- **Feature extraction** (e.g., detecting named entities in text, extracting edges in an image).
- **Model inference** (e.g., running a machine learning model on input data).
- **Decision-making** (e.g., routing execution based on confidence scores).

Nodes serve as **modular components**, allowing developers to design complex workflows by connecting them flexibly.

Types of Nodes

Nodes can be categorized based on their **role in an AI pipeline**:

Node Type	Description	Example
Input Node	Entry point of data into the pipeline	Ingesting user queries in a chatbot

Processing Node	Applies transformations to data	Tokenizing text, applying filters to images
Computation Node	Executes machine learning models	Running an LLM for text summarization
Decision Node	Implements branching logic based on conditions	Routing high-confidence results to an output node
Output Node	Final step that returns results	Sending generated responses to the user

Defining a Node in LangGraph

Nodes in LangGraph are defined as **functions** that process inputs and return outputs.

Python

python

```
import langgraph
```

```python
# Define a simple node

def preprocess_text(data):

    """Tokenizes text input into words."""

    return                       {"tokens":
data["text"].split()}


# Create a graph and add the node

graph = langgraph.Graph()

graph.add_node("preprocess_text",
preprocess_text)


# Execute the node

result = graph.run({"text": "Graph-based AI
pipelines are efficient."})

print(result)    #  Output:  {'tokens':
['Graph-based', 'AI', 'pipelines', 'are',
'efficient.']}
```

Explanation:

- The **preprocess_text** function tokenizes a string into words.
- This function is registered as a node in LangGraph.
- When executed, the node processes input data and returns structured output.

Nodes are fundamental to AI pipelines, but they do not operate in isolation—they need **edges** to define their relationships.

2. Edges: Connecting Nodes in an AI Pipeline

What is an Edge?

An **edge** represents a **directed connection** between two nodes, indicating the **flow of data and dependencies**. It determines **execution order** and how information is passed within the pipeline.

Types of Edges

Edges can have different behaviors based on **data flow and execution logic**:

Edge Type	Description	Example
Direct Edge	Passes output from one node to another	Tokenized text → Named entity recognition
Conditional Edge	Routes execution based on conditions	If confidence > 0.8 → Use model A, else use model B
Parallel Edge	Allows multiple nodes to execute simultaneously	Running sentiment analysis and translation in parallel
Loop Edge	Supports iterative execution	Reinforcement learning steps in AI training

Defining Edges in LangGraph

Edges define how **data flows** between nodes in LangGraph.

Python

python

```python
import langgraph

# Define nodes

def extract_text(data):

    """Extracts raw text from input."""

    return {"text": data["document"]}


def summarize_text(data):

    """Generates a short summary from text."""

    return {"summary": " ".join(data["text"].split()[:10])}


# Create a graph

graph = langgraph.Graph()
```

```python
graph.add_node("extract_text",
extract_text)

graph.add_node("summarize_text",
summarize_text)


# Add edges to connect nodes

graph.add_edge("extract_text",
"summarize_text")


# Execute the pipeline

input_data = {"document": "Graph-based AI
pipelines optimize execution efficiency."}

result = graph.run(input_data)


print(result)    #  Output:  {'summary':
'Graph-based   AI   pipelines   optimize
execution'}
```

Explanation:

- The **extract_text** node retrieves text from input.
- The **summarize_text** node generates a short summary.
- An **edge** connects these nodes, ensuring that the **output of extract_text becomes the input to summarize_text**.

Edges form the **logical pathways** of an AI pipeline, enforcing **task dependencies** that determine execution order.

---

3. Dependencies: Enforcing Execution Order

What are Dependencies?

A **dependency** defines **which nodes must complete execution before another node can run**. Dependencies ensure:

- **Correct ordering of operations** (e.g., preprocessing must happen before model inference).
- **Parallel execution** of independent tasks where possible.
- **Efficient resource utilization** by avoiding unnecessary computations.

Dependency Graphs in AI Pipelines

In a **dependency graph**, each node specifies **which other nodes must finish first** before it can execute.

Example Dependency Graph:

1. **Data Ingestion** → 2. **Preprocessing** → 3. **Feature Extraction**
2. **Model Training** → 5. **Hyperparameter Tuning**
3. **Inference** → 7. **Trained Model**

Nodes **(2, 3)** execute in parallel, while node **(4) waits for 3 and 5 to finish** before starting.

Implementing Dependencies in LangGraph

Dependencies are enforced by specifying **edges between nodes**.

Python

python

```python
import langgraph

# Define nodes

def clean_data(data):

    return            {"cleaned_text":
data["text"].lower()}  # Lowercasing text

def extract_features(data):
```

```python
    return                      {"features":
len(data["cleaned_text"].split())}  # Word
count


def classify_text(data):

    return  {"classification":  "Positive"
if data["features"] > 5 else "Negative"}


# Create a graph

graph = langgraph.Graph()

graph.add_node("clean_data", clean_data)

graph.add_node("extract_features",
extract_features)

graph.add_node("classify_text",
classify_text)


# Define dependencies

graph.add_edge("clean_data",
"extract_features")
```

```
graph.add_edge("extract_features",
"classify_text")


# Execute pipeline

input_data   =   {"text":   "Graph-based   AI
pipelines enhance workflow efficiency."}

result = graph.run(input_data)


print(result)  # Output: {'classification':
'Positive'}
```

Explanation:

- **clean_data** normalizes text.
- **extract_features** calculates word count (dependent on clean_data).
- **classify_text** makes a prediction (dependent on extract_features).

Dependencies enforce **correct execution order**, ensuring **logical workflow progression**.

3.3 Designing Scalable AI Workflows

Scalability is a critical factor in AI workflows, ensuring that pipelines can handle increasing data volumes, concurrent execution, and complex dependencies without performance degradation. **Graph-based AI workflows** offer a modular, parallelizable, and dynamic approach to AI pipeline design, enabling scalability across different use cases.

This chapter explores strategies for designing **scalable AI workflows** using LangGraph, covering **workflow architecture, parallel execution, state management, fault tolerance, and deployment strategies**. By the end of this chapter, you will be able to build AI workflows that efficiently scale from prototype to production.

---

1. Principles of Scalable AI Workflows

A **scalable AI workflow** exhibits the following characteristics:

1.1 Modularity

Workflows should be composed of **independent, reusable components** (nodes) that can be easily modified, replaced, or scaled without affecting the entire pipeline.

1.2 Parallelism

Tasks that do not depend on each other should run **in parallel** to maximize efficiency and reduce execution time.

1.3 Fault Tolerance

AI pipelines should gracefully **handle failures**, retry failed tasks, and ensure that errors do not halt the entire workflow.

1.4 Dynamic Execution

The pipeline should be capable of **adapting dynamically** based on conditions, optimizing execution paths, and skipping unnecessary computations.

1.5 Scalable State Management

Workflows should efficiently **manage intermediate states**, avoiding excessive memory usage while ensuring that necessary data is persisted.

These principles serve as the foundation for designing scalable AI workflows with LangGraph.

2. Workflow Architecture: Structuring Scalable Pipelines

A well-structured AI workflow follows a **modular, scalable architecture**. Below are the **three primary workflow patterns** used in AI systems:

2.1 Sequential Execution

A simple linear pipeline where each step **depends on the previous step**. This is common in data preprocessing and model inference pipelines.

Example: Sequential Workflow for Text Processing

Python

python

```
import langgraph

# Define nodes

def preprocess_text(data):

    return                          {"clean_text":
data["text"].lower()}


def extract_features(data):
```

```python
    return                    {"word_count":
len(data["clean_text"].split())}


def classify_text(data):

    return      {"label":      "Long"      if
data["word_count"] > 5 else "Short"}


# Create graph and add nodes

graph = langgraph.Graph()

graph.add_node("preprocess",
preprocess_text)

graph.add_node("extract",
extract_features)

graph.add_node("classify", classify_text)


# Define dependencies

graph.add_edge("preprocess", "extract")

graph.add_edge("extract", "classify")
```

```
# Execute workflow

result = graph.run({"text": "Graph-based AI
pipelines enhance scalability."})

print(result)  # Output: {'label': 'Long'}
```

Key Takeaway: Sequential execution is simple but **does not leverage parallelism**, making it inefficient for large-scale AI workflows.

2.2 Parallel Execution

Tasks that **do not depend on each other** can be executed in parallel, improving throughput.

Example: Parallel Sentiment Analysis and Translation

Python

python

```
import langgraph

def analyze_sentiment(data):
```

```python
    return {"sentiment": "Positive" if
"great" in data["text"] else "Neutral"}

def translate_text(data):

    return                       {"translated":
data["text"].replace("great",
"fantastic")}



# Create graph

graph = langgraph.Graph()

graph.add_node("sentiment",
analyze_sentiment)

graph.add_node("translate",
translate_text)



# No dependencies-both nodes execute in
parallel

graph.add_edge("input", "sentiment")

graph.add_edge("input", "translate")
```

```
# Execute workflow

result = graph.run({"text": "LangGraph is a
great tool!"})

print(result)      # Output:  {'sentiment':
'Positive', 'translated': 'LangGraph is a
fantastic tool!'}
```

Key Takeaway: Parallel execution speeds up processing by running independent tasks simultaneously.

2.3 Conditional Execution (Dynamic Workflows)

Conditional execution allows workflows to **adapt dynamically** based on runtime conditions.

Example: Dynamic Model Selection Based on Text Length

Python

python

```
import langgraph

def classify_text(data):

    if len(data["text"].split()) > 5:
```

```python
        return {"route": "detailed_model"}
    else:
        return {"route": "fast_model"}


def fast_model(data):
    return {"summary": data["text"][:30]}


def detailed_model(data):
    return {"summary": "Advanced summary of
text."}


# Create graph
graph = langgraph.Graph()
graph.add_node("classify", classify_text)
graph.add_node("fast_model", fast_model)
graph.add_node("detailed_model",
detailed_model)
```

```
# Conditional routing

graph.add_edge("classify",    "fast_model",
condition=lambda  data:  data["route"]  ==
"fast_model")

graph.add_edge("classify",
"detailed_model",  condition=lambda  data:
data["route"] == "detailed_model")



# Execute workflow

result  =  graph.run({"text":  "LangGraph
enables    efficient    and    scalable    AI
workflows."})

print(result)      #    Output:    {'summary':
'Advanced summary of text.'}
```

Key Takeaway: Dynamic workflows optimize execution paths by selecting appropriate branches based on conditions.

---

3. Managing State in Scalable Workflows

State management is critical in AI workflows that **track intermediate results across multiple nodes**. LangGraph provides mechanisms for **persistent and transient state management**.

3.1 Stateful Execution in LangGraph

Example: Caching Intermediate Results

Python

python

```python
import langgraph

# State dictionary

state = {}

def load_data(data):

    state["text"] = data["text"]

    return {"text": data["text"]}


def preprocess_text(data):

    state["clean_text"]                        =
data["text"].lower()

    return                    {"clean_text":
state["clean_text"]}
```

```python
def store_results(data):

    state["final_output"] = data

    return state


# Create graph

graph = langgraph.Graph()

graph.add_node("load", load_data)

graph.add_node("preprocess",
preprocess_text)

graph.add_node("store", store_results)


graph.add_edge("load", "preprocess")

graph.add_edge("preprocess", "store")


# Execute workflow

result = graph.run({"text": "Scalable AI
workflows with LangGraph!"})
```

```
print(state["final_output"])    # Cached
results
```

Key Takeaway: Stateful execution improves efficiency by persisting results and avoiding redundant computations.

---

4. Fault Tolerance and Error Handling

A **scalable AI pipeline must handle failures gracefully** to ensure continuous operation.

4.1 Implementing Retry Logic

Retries help **recover from transient failures**.

Python

python

```python
import random

def unreliable_task(data):

    if random.random() < 0.3:

        raise Exception("Random failure
occurred")
```

```python
    return {"result": "Success"}


# Retry mechanism

for _ in range(3):

    try:

        result = unreliable_task({})

        print(result)

        break

    except Exception as e:

        print(f"Retrying due to: {e}")
```

Key Takeaway: Retry logic prevents temporary failures from disrupting the entire pipeline.

Part 2: Practical AI Workflow Implementation

Chapter 4: Building a Basic AI Workflow with LangGraph

Building AI workflows efficiently requires a structured approach that integrates modular components, well-defined transitions, and scalable execution strategies. **LangGraph** provides a powerful framework for constructing AI workflows using **graph-based processing**, enabling flexible execution paths and optimized resource utilization.

This chapter offers a **step-by-step guide** to constructing a simple AI workflow with LangGraph, covering **node creation, transitions, debugging, and optimization techniques**. By the end of this chapter, you will have a **fully functional AI pipeline** and a deep understanding of how to design, troubleshoot, and refine AI graphs for production use.

4.1 Step-by-Step Guide to Creating a Simple AI Graph

AI workflows are becoming increasingly complex, requiring structured, scalable, and modular designs to handle real-world automation and decision-making tasks efficiently. **LangGraph** provides a robust framework for constructing AI workflows using a **graph-based approach**, enabling flexible execution paths, parallel processing, and dynamic transitions.

This chapter presents a **step-by-step guide** to designing a **simple AI graph** using LangGraph, covering **node creation, transitions, execution, and optimization**. By following this guide, you will gain hands-on experience in **constructing a fully functional AI pipeline**, laying the foundation for more complex workflows.

4.1.1 Understanding AI Graphs

An **AI workflow graph** consists of interconnected components that define how data flows through various processing steps. Unlike traditional procedural workflows, graph-based AI pipelines provide:

- **Modularity** – Each node performs a specific task, making workflows easier to manage and modify.
- **Scalability** – Parallel execution and dynamic branching improve performance.
- **Stateful Processing** – Intermediate results can be stored and reused throughout the workflow.

Key Components of an AI Graph

1. **Nodes** – Individual units of computation that perform operations (e.g., data preprocessing, inference, or post-processing).

2. **Edges (Transitions)** – Define execution flow between nodes, determining how data moves through the graph.
3. **Execution Context** – Maintains the current state of the workflow, ensuring that intermediate results persist as nodes process the input.

4.1.2 Setting Up the Development Environment

Before building an AI graph, ensure you have LangGraph and its dependencies installed.

Installing Required Packages

bash

```
pip install langgraph langchain openai
```

If using **OpenAI models**, set up your API key:

python

```
import os

os.environ["OPENAI_API_KEY"] = "your-api-key-here"
```

4.1.3 Designing a Basic AI Graph

Problem Statement

In this section, we will build a **basic AI workflow** that performs the following tasks:

1. **Receives user input** (a text query).
2. **Preprocesses the text** (converting it to lowercase and removing punctuation).
3. **Classifies intent** (determining if the input is a question or a statement).
4. **Generates a response** based on the intent.

Graph Structure

mathematica

```
Input  →  Preprocess  →  Classify Intent  →
Generate Response
```

This graph provides a **structured execution flow** for processing text-based queries, allowing dynamic responses based on intent classification.

4.1.4 Implementing the AI Graph in LangGraph

Step 1: Define Node Functions

Each **node** in the AI workflow graph performs a specific function.

Preprocessing Node

This node converts text to lowercase and removes punctuation.

python

```python
def preprocess_text(state):

    """Cleans the input text by converting
it to lowercase and removing
punctuation."""

    clean_text                              =
state["text"].lower().replace(".",
"").replace(",", "")

    return {"clean_text": clean_text}
```

Intent Classification Node

This node determines whether the input is a **question or a statement**.

python

```python
def classify_intent(state):

    """Classifies the input as a question
or a statement based on punctuation."""

    return {"intent": "question" if "?" in
state["clean_text"] else "statement"}
```

Response Generation Node

This node generates an appropriate response based on the classified intent.

python

```python
def generate_response(state):

    """Generates a response based on the
intent classification."""

    if state["intent"] == "question":

        return {"response": "That is an
interesting question. Let me help answer
it."}

    else:
```

```python
        return {"response": "Thank you for
your statement. I acknowledge it."}
```

Step 2: Construct the AI Graph

With the **node functions** defined, the next step is to construct the workflow graph using LangGraph.

python

```python
import langgraph

# Create a graph instance

graph = langgraph.Graph()

# Add nodes

graph.add_node("preprocess",
preprocess_text)

graph.add_node("classify",
classify_intent)

graph.add_node("response",
generate_response)
```

```python
# Define transitions (edges)

graph.add_edge("preprocess", "classify")

graph.add_edge("classify", "response")
```

In this setup:

- **Text preprocessing** occurs first.
- The **cleaned text** is passed to the **intent classification node**.
- The **classified intent** determines the **final response**.

Step 3: Execute the AI Workflow

Now, we execute the graph using an example input.

python

```python
# Run the workflow

result = graph.run({"text": "Is LangGraph useful?"})

print(result)  # Output: {'response': 'That is an interesting question. Let me help answer it.'}
```

4.1.5 Extending the AI Graph with Additional Features

Handling Multiple Processing Paths

We can modify the AI graph to handle **sentiment analysis** along with intent classification.

Sentiment Analysis Node

python

```python
def analyze_sentiment(state):

    """Determines if the text has a positive or negative sentiment."""

    return {"sentiment": "positive" if "good" in state["clean_text"] else "negative"}
```

Modifying the Graph to Include Sentiment Analysis

python

```python
graph.add_node("sentiment",
analyze_sentiment)


# Add sentiment analysis after
preprocessing
graph.add_edge("preprocess", "sentiment")

graph.add_edge("sentiment", "classify")
```

This **extends the graph**, allowing it to classify both **intent and sentiment**, enabling **more contextual responses**.

4.1.6 Debugging and Optimization Techniques

Debugging AI Workflows

When working with AI graphs, debugging is crucial for identifying issues.

1. Logging Outputs at Each Step

To inspect intermediate states, add logging:

python

```python
def debug_node(state):

    print("Current State:", state)

    return state
```

2. Running Individual Nodes for Testing

Each node can be **executed independently** for debugging.

python

```python
print(preprocess_text({"text": "Hello, how
are you?"}))
```

Optimizing Performance

1. **Parallel Execution** – Run independent nodes simultaneously to improve speed.
2. **Caching Results** – Store frequently used computations to reduce redundant processing.
3. **Minimizing Memory Usage** – Remove unnecessary variables after processing.

Example: **Deleting unused variables to optimize memory**

python

```python
def preprocess_text(state):

    clean_text = state["text"].lower()

    del state["text"]   # Remove original
text to save memory

    return {"clean_text": clean_text}
```

4.2 Implementing Basic Nodes and Transitions

In the previous section, we introduced **AI workflow graphs** and built a simple LangGraph-based AI pipeline. This chapter delves deeper into the **fundamental building blocks** of these workflows—**nodes and transitions**. Nodes define computational tasks, while transitions dictate the execution flow between these tasks.

This chapter will cover:

1. **Defining and implementing basic nodes** – Building different types of processing nodes.
2. **Understanding transitions** – Structuring execution paths between nodes.

3. **Handling conditional and parallel transitions** – Creating dynamic and scalable AI workflows.

4. **Best practices and debugging techniques** – Optimizing workflows for performance and reliability.

By the end of this section, you will have a solid grasp of **node construction and transition management**, enabling you to design more **robust and scalable AI pipelines**.

4.2.1 Understanding Nodes in LangGraph

Nodes are the **core processing units** of an AI workflow graph. Each node performs a **specific operation** (e.g., data preprocessing, classification, decision-making, or response generation).

Key Characteristics of Nodes

- **Stateless or Stateful** – Nodes can be **stateless** (processing data without memory) or **stateful** (retaining intermediate results).

- **Deterministic or Non-Deterministic** – Some nodes always return the same output for a given input, while others (e.g., those using LLMs) introduce randomness.

- **Single or Multi-Output** – Nodes may return a **single result** or **multiple possible outputs**, depending on the workflow design.

Defining a Basic Node

A node in LangGraph is typically implemented as a **Python function** that accepts input and returns output in a dictionary format.

python

```
def basic_node(state):

    """A simple node that transforms input text."""

    return                          {"output":
state["text"].upper()}  # Convert text to
uppercase
```

This **basic node** processes an input dictionary containing "text", modifies it, and returns an **updated state** with an "output" key.

4.2.2 Implementing Key Node Types

1. Data Preprocessing Node

A preprocessing node **cleans and normalizes** raw input before further processing.

python

```python
import re

def preprocess_text(state):

    """Cleans input text by removing
special characters and converting to
lowercase."""

    clean_text = re.sub(r"[^a-zA-Z0-9\s]",
"", state["text"]).lower()

    return {"clean_text": clean_text}
```

How It Works:

- Uses **regular expressions** to remove special characters.
- Converts text to **lowercase** for uniformity.

---

2. Decision-Making Node

Some workflows require **decision nodes** that classify or route data based on conditions.

python

```python
def classify_text(state):
```

```
"""Classifies text as either a question
or a statement."""

intent = "question" if "?" in
state["clean_text"] else "statement"

return {"intent": intent}
```

How It Works:

- Checks if the text **contains a question mark** to classify the input.
- Returns an **intent label**, which determines the **next processing step**.

---

3. External API Node (LLM Integration)

Many AI workflows involve **calling external models** (e.g., OpenAI, DeepSeek, or custom ML models).

python

```
from langchain.chat_models import
ChatOpenAI
```

```python
llm = ChatOpenAI(model="gpt-3.5-turbo")


def generate_response(state):

    """Uses an LLM to generate a response
based on the input."""

    prompt    =    f"Respond    to    this:
{state['clean_text']}"

    response = llm.predict(prompt)

    return {"response": response}
```

How It Works:

- Constructs a **prompt** based on the preprocessed text.
- Calls an **LLM** (e.g., OpenAI's GPT-3.5).
- Returns the **generated response**.

4.2.3 Understanding Transitions in LangGraph

Transitions define **execution flow** between nodes, ensuring data moves through the graph correctly.

Defining Transitions

Transitions are created using `graph.add_edge()` to **connect nodes** logically.

python

```
import langgraph

graph = langgraph.Graph()

# Add nodes

graph.add_node("preprocess",
preprocess_text)

graph.add_node("classify", classify_text)

graph.add_node("respond",
generate_response)


# Define transitions

graph.add_edge("preprocess", "classify")

graph.add_edge("classify", "respond")
```

How It Works:

- The **preprocessing node** runs first.

- The **classification node** receives the cleaned text.
- The **response node** generates a response based on classification.

4.2.4 Handling Conditional Transitions

Real-world workflows often **branch dynamically** based on intermediate results.

Example: Handling Different Intents

python

```python
def route_intent(state):
    """Routes execution based on intent."""
    if state["intent"] == "question":
        return "respond_question"
    else:
        return "respond_statement"
```

Updating the Graph with Conditional Transitions

python

```python
graph.add_node("route", route_intent)
```

```
graph.add_edge("classify", "route")


# Add response nodes

graph.add_node("respond_question", lambda
state: {"response": "Answering your
question..."})

graph.add_node("respond_statement", lambda
state: {"response": "Acknowledging your
statement."})


# Define conditional transitions

graph.add_conditional_edges("route",
route_intent)
```

How It Works:

- The **routing node** determines execution flow.
- **Different response nodes** handle **questions vs. statements**.

4.2.5 Implementing Parallel Transitions

Some workflows involve **multiple nodes running simultaneously** (e.g., **sentiment analysis and intent classification in parallel**).

Example: Running Multiple Analyses in Parallel

python

```python
def analyze_sentiment(state):

    """Determines sentiment polarity."""

    sentiment = "positive" if "good" in
state["clean_text"] else "negative"

    return {"sentiment": sentiment}
```

Modifying the Graph for Parallel Execution

python

```python
graph.add_node("sentiment",
analyze_sentiment)
```

```
# Run sentiment analysis and classification
in parallel

graph.add_edges("preprocess", ["classify",
"sentiment"])
```

How It Works:

- **Classification and sentiment analysis** run **simultaneously** after preprocessing.
- Results from **both nodes** are stored in the execution state.

4.2.6 Best Practices for Node and Transition Design

1. Keep Nodes Modular

Each node should **perform a single task** to enhance reusability and maintainability.

2. Optimize Execution Paths

Minimize **unnecessary transitions** to **reduce processing time**.

3. Implement Logging for Debugging

Add **intermediate logging** to track execution flow.

python

```python
def debug_node(state):

    print("Debug State:", state)

    return state
```

4. Use Error Handling for Robustness

Wrap external API calls with **error handling**.

python

```python
def generate_response_safe(state):

    try:

        return generate_response(state)

    except Exception as e:

        return {"error": str(e)}
```

4.3 Debugging and Optimization

As AI workflows grow in complexity, debugging and optimization become critical for ensuring **efficiency, reliability, and scalability**. Poorly designed pipelines can lead to **unexpected failures, high latency, and excessive resource consumption**, making debugging and optimization essential for building **production-ready AI applications**.

This chapter will cover:

1. **Debugging techniques for AI workflows** – Identifying and resolving issues in LangGraph-based pipelines.
2. **Logging and monitoring best practices** – Tracking workflow execution and diagnosing failures.
3. **Profiling and performance optimization** – Enhancing execution speed and resource efficiency.
4. **Scaling AI workflows** – Strategies for handling larger workloads and parallel execution.
5. **Common pitfalls and troubleshooting** – Addressing real-world issues in AI automation.

By the end of this chapter, you will be able to **debug, optimize, and scale** AI pipelines built with LangGraph and LangChain, ensuring they perform reliably in real-world environments.

4.3.1 Debugging Techniques for AI Workflows

Debugging AI pipelines requires a **structured approach** to isolate and resolve issues effectively. The key steps are:

1. **Identifying Failure Points** – Determining which node or transition is causing issues.
2. **Examining Execution State** – Analyzing intermediate data and logs.
3. **Reproducing the Issue** – Running tests in a controlled environment.
4. **Applying Fixes and Validating** – Implementing solutions and ensuring correctness.

Step 1: Identifying Failure Points

AI workflows in LangGraph execute **sequentially or in parallel**, making it crucial to identify which node or transition is failing. LangGraph provides **execution state tracking**, allowing developers to inspect **which node last executed** before failure.

Using Debugging Hooks

LangGraph allows setting up **event hooks** to capture execution data.

python

```python
def debug_node(state):
    """Logs the current state before processing."""
    print(f"Debugging Node: {state}")
    return state
```

To apply this debugging node to any part of the graph:

python

```python
graph.add_node("debug", debug_node)
graph.add_edge("preprocess", "debug")
```

This ensures **intermediate data** is logged before proceeding to the next step.

Step 2: Examining Execution State

LangGraph maintains a **state dictionary** throughout execution, which can be inspected for unexpected behavior.

Example: Printing State at Each Step

python

```python
def log_execution_state(state, step_name):
    """Logs execution state at a specific
step."""
    print(f"[{step_name}] State: {state}")
    return state
```

Incorporating this into a pipeline:

python

```python
graph.add_node("log_state", lambda state:
log_execution_state(state,
"Preprocessing"))

graph.add_edge("preprocess", "log_state")
```

This approach **tracks workflow progress**, helping identify where data gets corrupted or lost.

Step 3: Reproducing and Fixing the Issue

Once an issue is identified, **isolating it in a controlled environment** makes debugging more effective.

Example: Reproducing a LLM API Failure

If an AI workflow fails due to an LLM API call, testing the function separately helps pinpoint the issue.

python

```
from     langchain.chat_models     import
ChatOpenAI

llm = ChatOpenAI(model="gpt-3.5-turbo")


def test_llm():

    """Test LLM call separately."""

    try:

        response     =     llm.predict("Test
prompt")
```

```
        print("LLM Response:", response)

    except Exception as e:

        print("Error:", str(e))



test_llm()
```

By isolating and testing components separately, issues such as **invalid API keys, network failures, or incorrect response handling** can be resolved efficiently.

4.3.2 Logging and Monitoring Best Practices

Comprehensive logging and monitoring improve **observability** and **troubleshooting efficiency** in AI workflows.

1. Structured Logging

Instead of raw print statements, structured logging enhances **readability and searchability**.

python

```
import logging
```

```
logging.basicConfig(level=logging.INFO)

def log_node(state, node_name):

    logging.info(f"Node:         {node_name},
State: {state}")

    return state
```

2. Centralized Logging with LangChain Tracing

LangChain provides **built-in tracing** for tracking execution paths and latency.

python

```
import langchain

langchain.debug = True   # Enables tracing
logs
```

This **automatically logs** all interactions between nodes, helping debug **execution order and timing issues**.

4.3.3 Profiling and Performance Optimization

Optimizing AI workflows improves **speed, efficiency, and cost-effectiveness**.

1. Profiling Execution Time

Python's `time` module helps measure execution speed at each step.

python

```python
import time

def timed_node(state, step_name):

    start_time = time.time()

    result = state  # Simulate processing

    elapsed = time.time() - start_time

    print(f"{step_name}    Execution    Time:
{elapsed:.4f} seconds")

    return result
```

This helps identify **bottlenecks** that slow down AI pipelines.

2. Caching Expensive Operations

Reusing previous results prevents redundant computations.

python

```python
from functools import lru_cache

@lru_cache(maxsize=10)

def cached_llm_call(prompt):

    return llm.predict(prompt)
```

This prevents unnecessary LLM API calls, significantly **reducing costs** and **improving response time**.

---

3. Parallel Execution for Speedup

Running nodes in parallel improves throughput for tasks that **do not depend on each other**.

python

```python
graph.add_edges("preprocess", ["classify",
"sentiment_analysis"])
```

This ensures both nodes execute **simultaneously**, improving efficiency.

4.3.4 Scaling AI Workflows

As workflows handle larger workloads, scaling techniques improve **resilience and performance**.

1. Distributed Execution with Ray

Ray allows executing nodes **on multiple machines** for large-scale workloads.

python

```
from ray import remote

@remote

def parallel_node(state):

    return {"result": state["input"] * 2}
```

LangGraph can integrate with Ray for **distributed AI processing**, handling larger workloads seamlessly.

---

2. Queue-Based Execution for Stability

Using message queues (e.g., RabbitMQ, Kafka) **decouples execution**, preventing **overloading AI models**.

python

```
from kafka import KafkaProducer

producer                              =
KafkaProducer(bootstrap_servers="localhost
:9092")


def send_to_queue(state):

    producer.send("ai_pipeline",
value=state.encode())

    return {"status": "queued"}
```

This ensures **scalability and fault tolerance** in production workflows.

4.3.5 Common Pitfalls and Troubleshooting

1. Handling API Rate Limits

Most LLM providers impose **rate limits,** leading to failures.

Solution: Implement **exponential backoff** for retries.

python

```python
import time

def call_api_with_retry(api_call, max_retries=3):

    for attempt in range(max_retries):

        try:

            return api_call()

        except Exception as e:

            time.sleep(2 ** attempt)  # Exponential backoff

    return {"error": "API failed after retries"}
```

---

2. Preventing Infinite Loops

Loops in AI graphs can lead to **infinite execution**.

Solution: Implement **max execution depth** constraints.

python

```python
def controlled_loop(state, max_depth=5):

    if state.get("depth", 0) >= max_depth:

        return    {"error":    "Max    depth
reached"}

    return {"depth": state["depth"] + 1}
```

---

3. Debugging Inconsistent LLM Outputs

LLMs sometimes return **unexpected variations** in responses.

Solution: Enforce **temperature control** and **system prompts**.

python

```python
llm   =   ChatOpenAI(model="gpt-3.5-turbo",
temperature=0.2)     #   Lower   temperature
reduces randomness
```

Chapter 5: Integrating LangChain for Intelligent Agents

LangChain has emerged as a powerful framework for building **intelligent AI agents** that can **reason, interact with tools, retain memory, and dynamically adapt** to user inputs. By integrating LangChain with LangGraph, developers can construct **modular, scalable, and production-ready AI workflows** that go beyond simple LLM calls.

This chapter explores:

1. **LangChain's role in AI workflows** – How it extends LLMs with structured interactions.
2. **Connecting LLMs, tools, and memory** – Creating agents that leverage APIs, databases, and external knowledge.
3. **Use cases in RAG (Retrieval-Augmented Generation)** – Enhancing AI responses with real-world information.

By the end of this chapter, you will be able to **design, implement, and optimize** intelligent agents using LangChain and LangGraph, ensuring they perform effectively in real-world applications.

5.1 Understanding LangChain's Role in AI Workflows

Modern AI applications require more than just powerful language models—they need structured workflows that allow AI to **retrieve information, interact with external tools, remember past conversations, and reason effectively**. This is where **LangChain** plays a critical role.

LangChain is a **framework for building AI pipelines** that go beyond simple LLM-based text generation. It provides a structured way to integrate **memory, tool usage, decision-making, and data retrieval** into an AI system, making it more dynamic, responsive, and practical for real-world applications.

This section will explore:

1. **The limitations of standalone LLMs** and how LangChain overcomes them.
2. **Key components of LangChain** and how they fit into AI workflows.
3. **Real-world use cases** demonstrating LangChain's practical applications.

By the end of this chapter, you will have a strong foundational understanding of LangChain and how it **extends and enhances LLM capabilities** for **intelligent, structured AI agents**.

Why LangChain? The Limitations of Standalone LLMs

Large Language Models (LLMs) like **GPT-4** are incredibly powerful at **understanding and generating text**, but they **lack structure, memory, and external knowledge access**.

Here are some of the key **challenges** with using LLMs in real-world applications:

Limitation	Description	How LangChain Solves It
No Memory	LLMs do not remember previous interactions in a conversation. Each input is treated independently.	LangChain provides **memory modules** that retain conversational context across multiple turns.
No External Tools	LLMs cannot execute actions like fetching web data, querying databases,	LangChain enables integration with **APIs, search**

	or performing calculations.	**engines, and external tools.**
Limited Control Flow	LLMs follow **a single-pass approach**—they generate text without structured reasoning or decision-making.	LangChain introduces **agents** that dynamically choose which tools to use and how to respond.
Static Knowledge	LLMs are trained on **pre-existing data** and cannot access real-time information.	LangChain allows **retrieval-augmented generation (RAG)** to fetch **live and up-to-date** information.

By addressing these limitations, LangChain allows developers to create **AI-powered applications that are interactive, adaptable, and capable of executing complex workflows.**

LangChain's Core Components in AI Workflows

LangChain provides a modular framework that consists of **five primary components**, each playing a crucial role in building structured AI workflows.

1. LLMs: The Foundation

LLMs remain at the heart of any LangChain-based workflow. They **process user queries, generate responses, and execute reasoning tasks.** LangChain supports multiple models, including **OpenAI's GPT, Google's Gemini, and local models like Llama.**

Example: Initializing an LLM in LangChain

python

```
from     langchain.chat_models     import
ChatOpenAI

llm      =       ChatOpenAI(model="gpt-4",
temperature=0.5)  # Balanced creativity and
accuracy

response    =      llm.predict("What      is
LangChain?")

print(response)
```

This basic example **queries an LLM**, but in a real AI workflow, we need **additional components** to extend functionality.

---

2. Chains: Structuring AI Pipelines

A **chain** is a structured sequence of operations that an AI system follows. It can involve:

- **Prompt templates** for dynamic input generation.
- **Multiple LLM calls** in sequence.
- **Tool execution** for fetching external data.

Example: Creating a Simple Chain

python

```python
from langchain.chains import LLMChain

from langchain.prompts import PromptTemplate


prompt = PromptTemplate(

    input_variables=["topic"],

    template="Explain {topic} in simple
terms."
```

```
)
chain = LLMChain(llm=llm, prompt=prompt)
response = chain.run("Neural Networks")
print(response)
```

Here, we define a **structured AI workflow** where a user provides a **topic**, and the LLM generates a **concise explanation**.

3. Memory: Retaining Context in Conversations

LLMs **do not retain conversation history** by default. LangChain provides **memory modules** that allow agents to recall past interactions, leading to **coherent multi-turn conversations**.

Example: Adding Memory to a Conversational Agent

python

```
from        langchain.memory        import
ConversationBufferMemory

from        langchain.chains        import
ConversationChain


memory = ConversationBufferMemory()
```

```python
chat_agent = ConversationChain(

    llm=llm,

    memory=memory

)


# First interaction

print(chat_agent.run("Hello, my name is Alex."))


# Follow-up interaction, the AI remembers the name

print(chat_agent.run("What is my name?"))
```

This enables **stateful AI assistants** that remember past interactions, a critical feature for **chatbots, personal assistants, and customer support AI.**

4. Tools: Enabling External Interactions

AI agents need access to **external tools and APIs** to perform real-world tasks such as:

- **Fetching real-time data** (e.g., weather, stock prices).
- **Querying databases** for structured information.
- **Executing computations** using Python.

Example: Creating a Simple Tool for Math Calculations

python

```python
from langchain.tools import Tool

def simple_calculator(expression: str) ->
str:

    """Evaluates a math expression."""

    try:

        return str(eval(expression))

    except Exception as e:

        return f"Error: {str(e)}"


calculator_tool = Tool(
```

```
name="Calculator",

func=simple_calculator,

description="A          calculator          that
evaluates mathematical expressions."

)
```

AI agents can now **invoke tools** rather than relying on imperfect LLM-based calculations.

---

5. Agents: Dynamic Decision-Making

Unlike simple chains, **agents dynamically choose which tools to use**. This is essential for creating AI assistants that can:

- **Decide when to retrieve documents, use APIs, or recall memory.**
- **Plan multiple steps in an AI workflow.**
- **Interact with multiple data sources intelligently.**

Example: Creating an Agent That Uses a Tool

python

```
from langchain.agents import AgentType,
initialize_agent
```

```python
agent = initialize_agent(

    tools=[calculator_tool],

    llm=llm,


agent=AgentType.ZERO_SHOT_REACT_DESCRIPTIO
N,

    verbose=True

)


response = agent.run("What is 12 * 9?")

print(response)
```

Here, the **agent decides whether to use the calculator tool** or answer with the LLM alone.

Real-World Applications of LangChain in AI Workflows

LangChain is widely used across **various industries**, enabling AI-powered solutions such as:

1. **Enterprise AI Assistants** – AI-powered customer support bots that **retrieve relevant documents and answer queries**.
2. **Research & Knowledge Management** – AI models that **search large datasets** and generate insights.
3. **Finance & Healthcare** – AI agents that **retrieve up-to-date regulations, perform calculations, and analyze reports**.
4. **E-commerce Chatbots** – Agents that **fetch product information, answer FAQs, and assist with transactions**.

Each of these use cases leverages **memory, retrieval, and tool integration**, making LangChain essential for **production-grade AI systems**.

5.2 Connecting LLMs, Tools, and Memory

Building an effective AI workflow requires more than just a powerful language model. While LLMs are excellent at text generation, they need to **interact with external tools, remember past interactions, and retrieve relevant knowledge** to be truly useful.

LangChain provides a structured approach to achieving this by integrating three critical components:

1. **LLMs (Large Language Models)** – The core of AI reasoning and language generation.
2. **Tools** – External functions that allow LLMs to fetch data, perform calculations, or interact with APIs.
3. **Memory** – A mechanism that enables AI systems to maintain context and recall past interactions.

By **seamlessly connecting these elements**, LangChain transforms LLMs into intelligent, interactive AI agents capable of executing complex tasks.

In this chapter, we will:

- **Explore how LLMs interact with tools and memory** in LangChain.
- **Implement hands-on examples** of connecting LLMs with tools (such as APIs, databases, and web search).
- **Integrate memory modules** to enable long-term context retention.
- **Demonstrate a real-world AI pipeline** that combines all three elements.

By the end, you will have a strong understanding of how to build **structured, intelligent, and interactive AI workflows** using LangChain.

---

1. The Role of LLMs in an AI Workflow

An **LLM serves as the brain** of an AI application, responsible for:

- **Processing natural language input**
- **Generating meaningful responses**
- **Reasoning and making decisions**

However, LLMs have **three major limitations**:

1. **They lack real-time knowledge** – LLMs are trained on static datasets and cannot fetch live information.
2. **They cannot perform external tasks** – LLMs cannot execute API calls, run scripts, or query databases.
3. **They do not retain long-term memory** – LLMs treat each request independently without context from previous interactions.

Extending LLMs with LangChain

LangChain **overcomes these limitations** by providing:

- **Tools** to enable external interactions.
- **Memory** to retain conversational context.

- **Agents** to dynamically decide when and how to use tools.

Let's start by exploring how **tools** extend LLM functionality.

---

2. Integrating Tools for External Interactions

LangChain allows AI agents to **invoke tools** when they need additional capabilities. These tools can be used for:

- **Web search** – Retrieving real-time data.
- **API calls** – Fetching structured data from online services.
- **Calculations** – Performing mathematical operations.
- **Database queries** – Retrieving stored information.

Creating a Simple Tool: A Calculator

Let's start with a simple **math tool** that allows an LLM to perform calculations instead of relying on text-based approximations.

Implementation: Calculator Tool in LangChain

python

```
from langchain.tools import Tool

# Function to evaluate mathematical
expressions
```

```python
def simple_calculator(expression: str) ->
str:

    """Evaluates a math expression and
returns the result."""

    try:

        return str(eval(expression))

    except Exception as e:

        return f"Error: {str(e)}"


# Wrapping the function as a LangChain tool

calculator_tool = Tool(

    name="Calculator",

    func=simple_calculator,

    description="A    tool    to    evaluate
mathematical expressions."

)
```

Now, our AI agent can **invoke this tool when it needs to perform calculations.**

Connecting Tools to an LLM

We can create an **AI agent that decides when to use the calculator tool** instead of generating a response directly.

python

```
from langchain.chat_models import
ChatOpenAI

from langchain.agents import
initialize_agent, AgentType

# Initialize LLM

llm = ChatOpenAI(model="gpt-4",
temperature=0)

# Create an agent with the calculator tool

agent = initialize_agent(

    tools=[calculator_tool],

    llm=llm,
agent=AgentType.ZERO_SHOT_REACT_DESCRIPTIO
N,
```

```
    verbose=True

)

# Test the agent

response = agent.run("What is 25 * 4?")

print(response)
```

How It Works:

1. The agent **analyzes the query** and decides whether to call a tool or respond directly.
2. For math-related queries, it **invokes the calculator tool**.
3. The final answer is returned to the user.

This **modular approach** allows LLMs to **access real-world functionality** **without** **requiring** **retraining**.

---

3. Integrating Memory for Context Retention

Why Do AI Agents Need Memory?

By default, LLMs do not remember previous interactions. This creates issues such as:

- **Loss of conversation flow** – AI assistants forgetting user preferences.

- **Inability to track progress** – AI losing context in multi-step workflows.
- **Redundant queries** – AI asking users for information they already provided.

LangChain Memory Modules

LangChain provides different types of memory:

Memory Type	Description
ConversationBufferMemory	Stores recent messages as a history buffer.
ConversationSummaryMemory	Summarizes past interactions instead of storing full conversations.
ConversationKGMemory	Builds a knowledge graph of key concepts from conversations.

VectorStoreRetrieverMemory	Stores interactions as embeddings for long-term retrieval.

Implementing Conversation Memory

Here's how to integrate **ConversationBufferMemory** to enable context retention.

python

```python
from       langchain.memory       import
ConversationBufferMemory

from       langchain.chains       import
ConversationChain


# Initialize memory

memory = ConversationBufferMemory()


# Create a conversational AI agent with
memory

chat_agent = ConversationChain(
```

```
    llm=llm,

    memory=memory

)


# First interaction

print(chat_agent.run("Hello, my name is
Sarah."))


# Follow-up interaction

print(chat_agent.run("What is my name?"))
```

Expected Output:

pgsql

```
Hello, Sarah! How can I assist you today?

Your name is Sarah.
```

Now, the AI **remembers the user's name across multiple interactions**, making conversations more natural and fluid.

4. Building a Complete AI Workflow

Now that we have covered **LLMs, tools, and memory**, let's integrate them into a **fully functional AI agent** that:

1. **Maintains conversational memory**
2. **Uses external tools** when needed
3. **Dynamically decides when to use tools or generate responses**

Putting It All Together

python

```
from            langchain.memory         import
ConversationBufferMemory

from            langchain.agents         import
initialize_agent, AgentType


# Initialize LLM

llm         =          ChatOpenAI(model="gpt-4",
temperature=0)
```

```python
# Initialize memory
memory = ConversationBufferMemory()

# Create AI agent with tools and memory
agent = initialize_agent(
    tools=[calculator_tool],
    llm=llm,

agent=AgentType.CONVERSATIONAL_REACT_DESCR
IPTION,
    memory=memory,
    verbose=True
)

# Example conversation
print(agent.run("Hello, I am Alex."))
print(agent.run("What is 15 squared?"))
```

```
print(agent.run("Can you remind me of my
name?"))
```

What Happens Here?

1. The AI **greets the user and remembers their name**.
2. When asked a math question, it **calls the calculator tool** instead of generating an incorrect response.
3. The AI **recalls the user's name** from memory, demonstrating long-term context retention.

5.3 Use Cases in RAG (Retrieval-Augmented Generation)

Large Language Models (LLMs) are powerful, but they have a major limitation: their knowledge is **static** and **limited to their training data**. They cannot access **real-time** or **domain-specific** information unless explicitly provided. This is where **Retrieval-Augmented Generation (RAG)** comes into play.

RAG enhances LLMs by retrieving relevant external data at query time, making AI systems more dynamic, accurate, and context-aware. Instead of relying solely on pre-trained knowledge, RAG enables LLMs to **fetch up-to-date or proprietary information from structured and unstructured sources**.

In this chapter, we will:

- **Understand the fundamentals of RAG** and its role in AI workflows.
- **Explore practical use cases** where RAG significantly improves LLM applications.
- **Implement hands-on RAG examples** using LangChain, covering document retrieval, knowledge bases, and API-driven augmentation.
- **Discuss optimization techniques** to enhance retrieval accuracy, minimize latency, and scale production systems.

By the end of this chapter, you will be able to **build and deploy RAG-powered AI applications** that go beyond static knowledge, making them more **adaptive, reliable, and domain-specific**.

---

1. Understanding Retrieval-Augmented Generation (RAG)

What is RAG?

Retrieval-Augmented Generation (RAG) is a technique that combines:

1. **Retrieval** – Fetching relevant data from an external knowledge source (e.g., databases, APIs, document stores).

2. **Generation** – Using an LLM to synthesize a response based on both the retrieved data and its own reasoning capabilities.

How RAG Works

A **typical RAG workflow** consists of the following steps:

1. **User Query:** The AI system receives a question or request.
2. **Retrieval Step:** The system searches external knowledge sources (vector databases, APIs, or structured data) for relevant information.
3. **Augmentation:** The retrieved information is added as context to the prompt.
4. **Generation:** The LLM generates a response using both the retrieved knowledge and its own reasoning.
5. **Final Response:** The system returns the augmented response to the user.

Why is RAG Important?

RAG helps overcome **three major LLM limitations**:

Limitation	How RAG Helps
Lack of Real-Time Data	Retrieves up-to-date information from APIs or databases.

Domain-Specific Knowledge Gaps	Fetches enterprise knowledge from proprietary document stores.
Hallucination Issues	Reduces incorrect responses by grounding outputs in retrieved facts.

2. Practical Use Cases of RAG

RAG is widely used across industries to enhance AI applications. Below are key real-world **use cases** where RAG is essential.

2.1 Enterprise Knowledge Management

Use Case: Companies need AI assistants that understand their **internal documents, policies, and reports**.

Example: A legal firm uses an AI assistant that can retrieve **relevant legal clauses, past case studies, and compliance policies** when responding to client queries.

Implementation in LangChain

We can use **FAISS (Facebook AI Similarity Search)** as a **vector database** to store and retrieve enterprise knowledge.

python

```python
from langchain.vectorstores import FAISS

from langchain.embeddings.openai import
OpenAIEmbeddings

from langchain.document_loaders import
DirectoryLoader

from langchain.text_splitter import
RecursiveCharacterTextSplitter


# Load enterprise documents from a
directory

loader                                    =
DirectoryLoader("company_documents",
glob="*.txt")

documents = loader.load()


# Split documents into smaller chunks for
efficient retrieval
```

```
text_splitter                            =
RecursiveCharacterTextSplitter(chunk_size=
500, chunk_overlap=100)

docs                                     =
text_splitter.split_documents(documents)



# Create vector embeddings and store them
in FAISS

vectorstore   =   FAISS.from_documents(docs,
OpenAIEmbeddings())



# Save the vector database

vectorstore.save_local("enterprise_knowled
ge_base")
```

Now, whenever an employee asks a question, the system **retrieves the most relevant document sections** and augments the LLM's response with real company data.

2.2 Real-Time Data Retrieval (News, Finance, and Weather)

Use Case: AI chatbots need to access **live data** instead of relying on outdated training sets.

 Example: A finance chatbot retrieves the latest **stock market prices** before generating investment insights.

Implementation: Querying an API in LangChain

We can create a **retrieval tool** that fetches live stock data from an API before passing it to an LLM.

python

```python
import requests

from langchain.tools import Tool

# Function to retrieve real-time stock
price

def get_stock_price(symbol: str) -> str:
    url                              =
f"https://api.example.com/stocks/{symbol}"

    response = requests.get(url)

    return response.json()["price"]
```

```
# Create a LangChain tool

stock_price_tool = Tool(

    name="Stock Price Fetcher",

    func=get_stock_price,

    description="Fetches the latest stock
price for a given symbol."

)
```

This tool **retrieves live financial data** and allows the LLM to provide **real-time market insights** rather than static responses.

2.3 Customer Support with Contextual Memory

Use Case: AI-powered chatbots need to recall **past customer interactions** to provide personalized support.

Example: A telecom customer service bot retrieves **previous complaint history** before suggesting solutions.

Implementation: Connecting a CRM Database

We can use **SQL databases** to store and retrieve customer history for AI-based support systems.

python

```
from        langchain.utilities        import
SQLDatabase

# Connect to a CRM database

crm_db                                    =
SQLDatabase.from_uri("sqlite:///customer_d
ata.db")

# Retrieve a specific customer's past
interactions

query = "SELECT issue_description FROM
support_tickets WHERE customer_id = 12345"

customer_history = crm_db.run(query)


print(customer_history)
```

With this approach, AI chatbots can **personalize responses** based on customer history instead of treating every conversation as a new one.

2.4 Medical AI Assistants

Use Case: Doctors need AI assistants that retrieve **relevant medical literature and patient history** before providing recommendations.

Example: A clinical AI system fetches the **latest research papers and drug interactions** to assist doctors in treatment plans.

Implementation: Using PubMed for Medical Research

python

```python
from langchain.tools import WikipediaQueryRun

# Create a tool to retrieve medical literature

medical_research_tool = WikipediaQueryRun(api_wrapper="https://www.ncbi.nlm.nih.gov/pubmed/")
```

Now, the AI can **search medical research papers** and provide **evidence-based responses** instead of generic medical advice.

3. Optimizing RAG for Performance

To make RAG systems **fast and scalable**, consider the following optimizations:

Optimization	Benefit
Use a Fast Vector Database (FAISS, Pinecone, Weaviate)	Speeds up document retrieval.
Implement Hybrid Search (Semantic + Keyword Matching)	Improves accuracy of retrieved results.
Use Re-Ranking Models	Prioritizes the most relevant retrieved documents.
Precompute and Cache Results	Reduces redundant API calls and speeds up response times.

Chapter 6: Enhancing AI Workflows with External APIs and Databases

Modern AI applications require access to real-world data for dynamic interactions, contextual awareness, and improved decision-making. By integrating AI models with **external APIs** and **databases**, developers can build intelligent, adaptable, and scalable AI workflows. This chapter explores how to connect AI models with real-time data sources, leverage vector databases for semantic search, and use APIs for dynamic information retrieval.

6.1 Connecting AI Models to Real-World Data

Artificial Intelligence models become significantly more powerful when they can interact with **real-world data sources**. Static AI models, while useful for many applications, lack the ability to adapt to **changing environments, real-time events, and dynamic user inputs**. By integrating AI models with external **APIs, databases, and live data feeds**, developers can build applications that are **more intelligent, responsive, and context-aware**.

This section will explore how to connect AI models to real-world data using **LangChain and LangGraph**, covering:

1. The importance of real-world data integration in AI workflows

2. How to use APIs to fetch live data for AI applications
3. Implementing AI agents that dynamically call APIs
4. Handling structured and unstructured data efficiently
5. Best practices for building production-ready AI pipelines

6.1.1 Why AI Needs Real-World Data

Challenges of Static AI Models

Traditional AI models operate on **pre-trained knowledge** and **historical datasets**. However, in **many real-world applications**, static AI has limitations:

- **Outdated Information** – Pre-trained models cannot access recent events, breaking applications that rely on current data.
- **Lack of Personalization** – Models cannot adapt to users' changing preferences or behaviors.
- **Limited Decision-Making** – Without real-time data, AI models make decisions based on incomplete knowledge.

Benefits of Real-World Data Integration

By integrating **external APIs, databases, and live data sources**, AI models can:

- **Retrieve dynamic information** (e.g., stock prices, weather updates, news articles).

- **Interact with external systems** (e.g., CRM tools, financial services, IoT devices).
- **Enhance personalization** by adapting responses based on user interactions.
- **Improve reasoning and decision-making** with up-to-date knowledge.

6.1.2 Fetching Real-Time Data from APIs

Understanding APIs in AI Workflows

APIs (Application Programming Interfaces) allow AI models to communicate with **external data sources**. APIs provide:

- **Structured Data** – JSON or XML responses containing relevant information.
- **Unstructured Data** – Text, images, or documents retrieved from web services.
- **Transactional Capabilities** – Booking a flight, processing payments, or updating databases.

Types of APIs for AI Applications

- **Public APIs** – OpenWeather, NewsAPI, CoinGecko, Wikipedia
- **Private APIs** – Internal company APIs, financial data feeds

- **GraphQL APIs** – Custom queries to retrieve structured data efficiently
- **Streaming APIs** – Real-time data streams (e.g., WebSockets, Kafka)

6.1.3 Implementing API Calls in AI Pipelines

Example: Fetching Live Weather Data Using LangChain

The following example demonstrates how to use an **external API** in a LangChain-powered AI agent.

Python

python

```python
import requests

from langchain.tools import Tool

def fetch_weather(city):

    """Fetches real-time weather data for a given city."""

    api_key = "your_api_key"
```

```python
    url = f"https://api.openweathermap.org/data/2.5/weather?q={city}&appid={api_key}&units=metric"

    response = requests.get(url)

    data = response.json()

    return f"The weather in {city} is {data['weather'][0]['description']} with a temperature of {data['main']['temp']}°C."


# Wrap the function as a LangChain tool
weather_tool = Tool(

    name="WeatherAPI",

    func=fetch_weather,

    description="Fetches real-time weather information."

)
# Example call
print(fetch_weather("New York"))
```

Explanation:

1. **Requests API** fetches live weather data.
2. **LangChain's** `Tool` wraps the function for integration into AI pipelines.
3. The AI agent can now query real-time weather dynamically.

6.1.4 AI Agents That Interact with APIs

Building a Dynamic AI Agent with LangChain

AI models can be enhanced by **autonomously calling APIs** based on user queries.

Example: AI Agent That Fetches Cryptocurrency Prices

Python

python

```
from langchain.agents import AgentType,
initialize_agent

from langchain.llms import OpenAI

from langchain.tools import Tool
```

```python
def get_crypto_price(crypto_symbol):

    """Fetches   real-time   cryptocurrency
prices."""

    url                                    =
f"https://api.coingecko.com/api/v3/simple/
price?ids={crypto_symbol}&vs_currencies=us
d"

    response = requests.get(url)

    data = response.json()

    return   f"The   current   price   of
{crypto_symbol}                          is
${data[crypto_symbol]['usd']}."


# Wrap function in a LangChain tool

crypto_tool = Tool(

    name="CryptoPriceAPI",

    func=get_crypto_price,
```

```python
    description="Retrieves          real-time
cryptocurrency prices."

)


# Create AI agent

llm = OpenAI(temperature=0)

agent = initialize_agent(

    tools=[crypto_tool],

    llm=llm,


agent=AgentType.ZERO_SHOT_REACT_DESCRIPTIO
N,

    verbose=True

)


# Query the agent

agent.run("What is the price of bitcoin?")
```

Key Takeaways:

- The **agent autonomously calls APIs** based on user queries.
- **Real-time price retrieval** ensures AI remains accurate and up-to-date.
- The **LangChain agent framework** handles tool integration dynamically.

6.1.5 Handling Structured vs. Unstructured Data

AI workflows need to handle both **structured** and **unstructured** data from external sources.

Structured Data (JSON, XML, SQL Databases)

Example: API returns **JSON-formatted** stock prices.

json

```
{

    "AAPL": {

        "price": 183.23,

        "change": -0.5

    }
```

}

AI pipelines can parse and use this data efficiently.

Unstructured Data (News Articles, PDFs, Audio Transcripts)

Example: AI retrieves and processes text from a **news API**.

python

```
from langchain.document_loaders import NewsAPI

news_loader = NewsAPI(api_key="your_api_key")

articles = news_loader.load("AI advancements")

print(articles[0].text)
```

AI models must **preprocess, clean, and convert** unstructured data before using it.

6.1.6 Best Practices for Real-World Data Integration

1. API Rate Limiting & Error Handling

Many APIs have **rate limits**. Always include **error handling** in API requests.

Python

python

```python
import time

def safe_fetch(url):

    for _ in range(3):  # Retry mechanism

        response = requests.get(url)

        if response.status_code == 200:

            return response.json()

        time.sleep(2)

    return None  # Return None after retries fail
```

2. Caching API Responses for Efficiency

For frequently requested data, **cache responses** to reduce API calls.

Python

python

```
from cachetools import cached, TTLCache

cache = TTLCache(maxsize=100, ttl=300)  #
Cache for 5 minutes


@cached(cache)

def fetch_data(url):

    return requests.get(url).json()
```

3. Secure API Key Management

Never hardcode API keys in code. Use **environment variables** instead.

Python

python

```
import os

api_key = os.getenv("OPENAI_API_KEY")
```

6.2 Using Vector Databases with LangChain

Vector databases are a critical component of **modern AI workflows**, enabling efficient storage, retrieval, and similarity search of high-dimensional data. As AI models generate and process increasingly large amounts of text, images, and embeddings, traditional databases struggle with **semantic search, large-scale retrieval, and real-time querying**. Vector databases solve these challenges by providing **fast and efficient nearest-neighbor search**, making them essential for applications such as **retrieval-augmented generation (RAG), recommendation systems, and intelligent search engines**.

This section will explore:

1. What vector databases are and why they are essential in AI workflows
2. How vector embeddings work and their role in AI pipelines
3. How to integrate vector databases with LangChain for retrieval and search
4. Implementing real-world AI applications using LangChain and vector stores

5. Best practices for optimizing and scaling vector-based retrieval systems

---

6.2.1 Understanding Vector Databases

What Are Vector Databases?

A **vector database** is a specialized type of database optimized for storing and searching **vector embeddings**, which are numerical representations of data points in high-dimensional space. Unlike traditional relational databases that rely on structured queries (e.g., SQL), vector databases excel at **similarity search**, allowing AI models to retrieve semantically relevant information efficiently.

Why Are Vector Databases Important?

- **Fast Similarity Search** – Finds the most relevant documents based on meaning, not just keywords.
- **Scalability** – Efficiently handles millions of embeddings for large-scale applications.
- **Improved AI Responses** – Enhances AI models by enabling retrieval-augmented generation (RAG).
- **Multi-Modal Search** – Supports text, images, audio, and more.

Common Use Cases

- **Retrieval-Augmented Generation (RAG)** – Enhancing LLMs with external knowledge.
- **Semantic Search** – AI-powered search engines retrieving contextually relevant results.
- **Recommendation Systems** – Personalized content recommendations based on similarity.
- **Anomaly Detection** – Identifying unusual patterns in high-dimensional datasets.

6.2.2 How Vector Embeddings Work

What Are Embeddings?

Embeddings are **numerical representations** of text, images, or other data, capturing their meaning in a way that allows for **semantic comparisons**. In AI workflows, embeddings transform unstructured data into structured numerical vectors.

Example: Text Embeddings

A sentence like **"AI is transforming industries"** can be converted into a **dense vector representation**, such as:

plaintext

```
[-0.123, 0.785, -0.332, ..., 0.672]
```

The model learns that **"AI revolutionizes businesses"** has a similar vector, enabling **semantic similarity search** rather than exact keyword matching.

Generating Embeddings with LangChain

LangChain provides **embedding models** to convert text into vectors.

Python

python

```python
from langchain.embeddings import OpenAIEmbeddings


# Initialize the OpenAI embeddings model

embeddings = OpenAIEmbeddings()


# Convert text into a vector
```

```
vector = embeddings.embed_query("What is
artificial intelligence?")

print(vector[:5])  # Print first 5 values
for brevity
```

Key Takeaways:

- **Embeddings capture semantic meaning** rather than exact words.
- **Embedding models** (like OpenAI, BERT, or Cohere) generate high-dimensional vectors.
- **Vector databases store these embeddings** for efficient retrieval.

6.2.3 Storing and Retrieving Data with Vector Databases

Popular Vector Databases

Several specialized databases are optimized for storing and querying embeddings:

- **FAISS (Facebook AI Similarity Search)** – High-performance, optimized for large-scale retrieval.

- **Pinecone** – Fully managed, real-time search capabilities.
- **Weaviate** – Open-source, multi-modal search with extensive integrations.
- **ChromaDB** – Lightweight, developer-friendly vector store.

Example: Using FAISS for Storing Embeddings

FAISS is widely used for efficient similarity search.

Python

python

```python
import faiss

import numpy as np

# Create a sample dataset of vectors

dimension = 128  # Size of each embedding

index = faiss.IndexFlatL2(dimension)  # L2
distance for similarity search


# Generate random vectors (simulating
embeddings)

vectors    =    np.random.random((1000,
dimension)).astype('float32')
```

```python
# Add vectors to the FAISS index

index.add(vectors)


# Perform a search using a sample query
vector

query_vector    =    np.random.random((1,
dimension)).astype('float32')

distances,           indices             =
index.search(query_vector, k=5)  # Retrieve
top 5 similar vectors

print("Closest vectors:", indices)
```

Explanation:

1. **FAISS creates an index** to store vector embeddings.
2. **Embeddings are added** to the index.
3. **A search query retrieves similar vectors** based on distance metrics.

6.2.4 Integrating Vector Databases with LangChain

LangChain supports multiple vector databases for seamless **document retrieval and search**.

Example: Storing and Searching Documents with Pinecone

Python

python

```python
from langchain.vectorstores import Pinecone

from langchain.embeddings import OpenAIEmbeddings

import pinecone


# Initialize Pinecone

pinecone.init(api_key="your_pinecone_api_key", environment="us-west1-gcp")


# Define the index name
```

```python
index_name = "ai-docs"

# Create an embedding model

embedding_model = OpenAIEmbeddings()

# Initialize Pinecone vector store

vector_store = Pinecone.from_texts(
    texts=["AI       is       transforming
industries.", "Machine learning is a subset
of AI."],
    embedding=embedding_model,
    index_name=index_name
)


# Perform a similarity search

query = "How is AI impacting businesses?"

result                                     =
vector_store.similarity_search(query, k=2)

print(result)
```

Key Takeaways:

- **Pinecone stores embeddings** and allows fast retrieval.
- **LangChain simplifies integration** with vector databases.
- **Semantic search retrieves meaningful documents**, not just keyword matches.

6.2.5 Implementing a RAG System with LangChain and Vector Databases

Retrieval-Augmented Generation (RAG) Overview

RAG enhances language models by retrieving relevant **external documents** before generating responses.

Example: RAG with LangChain and FAISS

Python

python

```python
from langchain.chains import RetrievalQA

from langchain.llms import OpenAI

from langchain.vectorstores import FAISS
```

```python
from langchain.embeddings import OpenAIEmbeddings

from langchain.document_loaders import TextLoader


# Load documents

documents = ["AI is revolutionizing healthcare.", "Deep learning powers computer vision."]

embedding_model = OpenAIEmbeddings()


# Store documents in FAISS

vector_store = FAISS.from_texts(documents, embedding_model)


# Create a retrieval-based QA system

retriever = vector_store.as_retriever()
```

```
qa_chain                              =
RetrievalQA.from_chain_type(llm=OpenAI(),
retriever=retriever)


# Ask a question

response   =   qa_chain.run("How   is   AI
impacting healthcare?")

print(response)
```

How It Works:

1. **Documents are embedded** and stored in a **FAISS vector store**.
2. **User queries retrieve relevant documents** before generating responses.
3. **LangChain's RetrievalQA** uses the retrieved data to enhance AI responses.

6.2.6 Best Practices for Optimizing Vector-Based Retrieval

1. Choosing the Right Distance Metric

- **L2 (Euclidean Distance)** – Measures direct vector distance.
- **Cosine Similarity** – Measures **angle-based similarity** for text embeddings.

2. Indexing Techniques for Scalability

- **Hierarchical Navigable Small World (HNSW)** – Optimized for large-scale search.
- **IVFFlat (Inverted File Indexing)** – Efficient for large datasets.

3. Data Preprocessing for Better Embeddings

- **Remove stopwords and redundant text** to improve embedding quality.
- **Normalize data formats** for consistent representation.

6.3 API Integration for Dynamic Data Retrieval

APIs are fundamental to modern AI workflows, enabling dynamic access to real-time data from external sources such as **databases, web services, financial markets, IoT devices, and more**. By integrating APIs with LangChain, AI applications can **retrieve live data, enhance model responses, automate workflows, and**

perform intelligent decision-making based on constantly updated information.

This chapter will cover:

1. **Understanding API integration in AI workflows**
2. **Making API calls using LangChain tools**
3. **Processing and structuring retrieved data for AI applications**
4. **Building real-world use cases such as financial data retrieval, news aggregation, and live customer support**
5. **Best practices for optimizing API requests and handling rate limits**

6.3.1 Understanding API Integration in AI Workflows

What Is API Integration?

An **Application Programming Interface (API)** allows systems to communicate and exchange data. APIs can be **RESTful, GraphQL, WebSockets, or gRPC-based**, but for AI workflows, **REST APIs** are the most common.

APIs enable **AI models** to:

- **Access real-time information** (e.g., stock prices, weather, breaking news).
- **Retrieve domain-specific knowledge** (e.g., medical data, legal texts).
- **Integrate with enterprise systems** (e.g., CRMs, chatbots, customer support tools).
- **Automate decision-making processes** based on live data.

6.3.2 Making API Calls in LangChain

LangChain provides **API tools** that allow models to dynamically query APIs. These tools handle:

- **Fetching data from external sources**
- **Parsing responses**
- **Integrating results into AI pipelines**

Example: Basic API Call with LangChain

Let's retrieve real-time weather data using the OpenWeather API.

Python

python

```
from langchain.tools import RequestsGetTool
```

```python
# Define the API endpoint

api_key = "your_openweather_api_key"

city = "New York"

url = f"https://api.openweathermap.org/data/2.5/weather?q={city}&appid={api_key}&units=metric"


# Initialize LangChain API tool

weather_tool = RequestsGetTool()


# Fetch data from API

response = weather_tool.run(url)

print(response)
```

Explanation:

1. **Constructs an API request** to fetch live weather data.

2. **Uses LangChain's** `RequestsGetTool` to make a GET request.

3. **Retrieves and displays the JSON response**.

6.3.3 Processing API Responses for AI Applications

APIs typically return **JSON** responses, which must be parsed and structured before being used in an AI model.

Example: Parsing API Response

Python

python

```python
import json

# Sample API response

response_json = '''
{
  "weather":    [{"description":    "clear
sky"}],

  "main": {"temp": 22.5, "humidity": 55},
```

```
    "wind": {"speed": 3.6}

}

'''


# Convert to Python dictionary

data = json.loads(response_json)


# Extract relevant data

weather                                        =
data["weather"][0]["description"]

temperature = data["main"]["temp"]

humidity = data["main"]["humidity"]


print(f"Weather: {weather}, Temperature:
{temperature}°C, Humidity: {humidity}%")
```

Key Takeaways:

- **JSON responses must be parsed** before integration.

- **Only relevant fields** should be extracted for use in AI workflows.
- **Data cleaning and preprocessing** may be needed for consistency.

6.3.4 API Integration in Real-World AI Applications

Use Case 1: Retrieving Financial Data for AI-Driven Predictions

Live financial data can be used in **AI trading models, market trend analysis, and risk assessment.**

Example: Fetching Stock Market Data Using Alpha Vantage API

Python

python

```
from           langchain.tools          import
RequestsGetTool


api_key = "your_alpha_vantage_api_key"
```

```python
symbol = "AAPL"

url = f"https://www.alphavantage.co/query?function=TIME_SERIES_INTRADAY&symbol={symbol}&interval=5min&apikey={api_key}"


# Fetch stock market data

stock_tool = RequestsGetTool()

response = stock_tool.run(url)

print(response)
```

How It Works:

1. **Connects to a real-time stock market API.**
2. **Retrieves intraday stock prices for a given symbol.**
3. **Enables AI models to analyze trends dynamically.**

Use Case 2: AI-Powered News Aggregation

Integrating real-time news allows AI models to **fetch breaking stories, summarize headlines, and provide contextual insights**.

Example: Fetching News Using NewsAPI

Python

python

```python
from langchain.tools import RequestsGetTool


api_key = "your_newsapi_key"

url = f"https://newsapi.org/v2/top-headlines?country=us&apiKey={api_key}"


# Fetch news articles

news_tool = RequestsGetTool()

response = news_tool.run(url)

print(response)
```

Potential Applications:

- **Summarizing news articles** for AI-powered content generation.
- **Tracking real-time events** for decision-making.
- **Integrating current affairs into chatbots and virtual assistants.**

Use Case 3: AI-Enhanced Customer Support with External Knowledge Retrieval

APIs can be used to retrieve **real-time customer data, FAQs, or product details** for AI-powered assistants.

Example: Fetching Customer Data from a CRM System

Python

python

```
customer_id = "12345"

crm_api_url                                =
f"https://crm.example.com/api/customers/{c
ustomer_id}?api_key=your_api_key"
```

```python
# Fetch customer profile

customer_tool = RequestsGetTool()

customer_data                          =
customer_tool.run(crm_api_url)

print(customer_data)
```

Benefits:

- **Personalized AI responses** based on live customer data.
- **Automated customer interactions** using AI-driven chatbots.
- **Integration with support ticketing systems** for intelligent query handling.

6.3.5 Best Practices for API Integration in AI Workflows

1. Handling API Rate Limits

Most APIs enforce rate limits. **To avoid throttling:**

- **Use exponential backoff** when retrying failed requests.
- **Cache responses** when possible to reduce API calls.

- **Batch requests** to minimize API load.

Example: Handling API Rate Limits Python

python

```
import time

import requests

api_url = "https://api.example.com/data"

headers = {"Authorization": "Bearer
your_token"}

def fetch_data():

    for attempt in range(3):  # Retry up to
3 times

        response = requests.get(api_url,
headers=headers)

        if response.status_code == 429:  #
Too many requests

            wait_time = 2 ** attempt  #
Exponential backoff
```

```python
            print(f"Rate limited. Retrying
in {wait_time} seconds...")

            time.sleep(wait_time)

        else:

            return response.json()

    return None


data = fetch_data()
```

2. Securing API Keys

- **Store API keys securely** using environment variables.
- **Avoid hardcoding credentials** in source code.

Example: Using Environment Variables for API Keys Python

python

```python
import os

api_key = os.getenv("API_KEY")
```

3. Optimizing API Responses for AI Pipelines

- **Filter unnecessary fields** to reduce processing time.
- **Normalize and structure data** before feeding it into AI models.

Part 3: Hands-on Real-World Projects

Chapter 7: Project 1 – Automated Document Processing System

Automated document processing is essential in **legal, financial, healthcare, and enterprise sectors** where large volumes of unstructured data must be extracted, analyzed, and structured efficiently. This project will walk through building an **AI-driven document processing system using LangChain and LangGraph** to extract insights from **PDFs and text files**, process data through a **multi-step AI pipeline**, and deploy a **scalable, optimized system** for real-world applications.

7.1 Extracting Information from PDFs and Text Files

In modern AI applications, extracting and processing information from **unstructured documents** is a critical step in building intelligent automation systems. PDFs and text files are widely used in legal, financial, and enterprise settings, where extracting structured insights can streamline workflows, reduce manual effort, and enable advanced AI-driven decision-making.

This section explores how to extract and preprocess text from **PDF and TXT files** using **LangChain and Python-based tools**. The goal is to develop a **robust document ingestion pipeline** that can be seamlessly integrated into an **AI workflow with LangGraph** for further processing.

Understanding Document Processing in AI

Organizations deal with vast amounts of **unstructured text data** in various formats, including:

- **PDFs** (legal contracts, invoices, reports)
- **TXT files** (logs, transcripts, documentation)
- **Scanned documents** (OCR-based processing)

The process of extracting information from these formats involves multiple steps:

1. **Reading the file format (PDF, TXT, etc.)**
2. **Extracting raw text content**
3. **Cleaning and preprocessing the extracted text**
4. **Identifying key entities and insights**
5. **Structuring data for downstream AI processing**

Extracting Text from PDFs and Text Files Using LangChain

Working with PDFs

LangChain provides built-in tools to extract text from **searchable PDFs** efficiently.

Using PyMuPDF (fitz) for PDF Extraction

Python

python

```python
import fitz  # PyMuPDF

def extract_text_from_pdf(pdf_path):
    """Extracts text from a given PDF file."""

    doc = fitz.open(pdf_path)

    text = ""

    for page in doc:

        text += page.get_text() + "\n"  # Extract text from each page

    return text.strip()


# Example usage
pdf_text = extract_text_from_pdf("sample_document.pdf")
```

```
print(pdf_text[:500])  # Display the first
500 characters
```

Key Takeaways:

- `fitz.open()` **reads the PDF file** and extracts text page by page.
- **Handles searchable PDFs efficiently** but does not process scanned documents (requires OCR).

Using LangChain's PyMuPDFLoader for PDF Extraction

LangChain provides a higher-level interface to **ingest documents** efficiently.

Python

python

```
from   langchain.document_loaders   import
PyMuPDFLoader

loader                                =
PyMuPDFLoader("sample_document.pdf")

documents = loader.load()

# Display extracted content

for doc in documents:
```

```
print(doc.page_content[:500])
```

Advantages of using LangChain document loaders:

- **Unified document ingestion** for AI pipelines.
- **Integration with AI models, embeddings, and vector stores.**

Working with Text Files

Reading and Extracting Text from TXT Files

Text files are simpler to process than PDFs.

Python

python

```python
def extract_text_from_txt(txt_path):

    """Reads a text file and returns its content."""

    with open(txt_path, "r", encoding="utf-8") as file:

        return file.read()
```

```
# Example usage

txt_text                                =
extract_text_from_txt("sample_text.txt")

print(txt_text[:500])  # Display first 500
characters
```

- **Handles structured and unstructured text from logs, transcripts, and reports.**
- **Easier to preprocess compared to PDFs.**

Preprocessing and Cleaning Extracted Text

Once extracted, text **must be cleaned** before AI models process it. This includes:

- **Removing extra whitespace, special characters, and formatting artifacts.**
- **Standardizing text for further processing.**

Python

python

```
import re
```

```python
def clean_text(text):

    """Cleans extracted text by removing
    unnecessary whitespace and special
    characters."""

    text = re.sub(r"\s+", " ", text)   #
Remove extra spaces

    text = re.sub(r"[^\x00-\x7F]+", " ",
text)  # Remove non-ASCII characters

    return text.strip()


# Example usage

cleaned_text = clean_text(pdf_text)

print(cleaned_text[:500])
```

Key Optimizations:

- **Removes unwanted whitespace and formatting issues.**
- **Ensures compatibility with AI models by removing non-ASCII artifacts.**

Handling Scanned PDFs with OCR

Scanned documents contain text **embedded as images**, requiring Optical Character Recognition (OCR) for extraction.

Using Tesseract OCR for Text Extraction

Tesseract OCR is a powerful open-source tool for **recognizing text in scanned PDFs and images**.

Installation:

bash

```bash
pip install pytesseract pillow pdf2image
```

Extracting text from scanned PDFs: Python

python

```python
import pytesseract

from pdf2image import convert_from_path

from PIL import Image
```

```python
def
extract_text_from_scanned_pdf(pdf_path):

    """Extracts  text  from  scanned  PDFs
using Tesseract OCR."""

    images = convert_from_path(pdf_path)

    text = ""

    for image in images:

        text                               +=
pytesseract.image_to_string(image) + "\n"

    return text.strip()



# Example usage

ocr_text                                   =
extract_text_from_scanned_pdf("scanned_doc
ument.pdf")

print(ocr_text[:500])
```

Key Features:

- **Extracts text from image-based PDFs** where direct text extraction fails.

- **Useful for invoices, receipts, and handwritten documents.**

Structuring Extracted Text for AI Processing

Extracted text is often **unstructured** and needs to be structured for AI workflows.

Splitting Text into Chunks for AI Models

Large text documents need to be **split into smaller chunks** for AI processing.

Python

python

```
from    langchain.text_splitter    import
RecursiveCharacterTextSplitter

def    split_text(text,    chunk_size=500,
chunk_overlap=50):

    """Splits text into smaller chunks for
AI processing."""
```

```
    text_splitter                          =
RecursiveCharacterTextSplitter(chunk_size=
chunk_size, chunk_overlap=chunk_overlap)

    return text_splitter.split_text(text)


# Example usage

text_chunks = split_text(cleaned_text)

print(text_chunks[:3])   # Display first 3
chunks
```

Advantages:

- **Prepares text for AI summarization, question answering, and embeddings.**
- **Prevents exceeding token limits in models like GPT-4.**

Real-World Applications of Automated Text Extraction

1. Legal Document Processing

- Extract clauses, terms, and obligations from contracts.

- Automate due diligence and compliance checks.

2. Financial Report Analysis

- Extract financial metrics, trends, and anomalies.
- Automate earnings report summarization.

3. Medical Records Processing

- Extract patient information from scanned prescriptions.
- Automate clinical trial data extraction.

4. Log File Analysis

- Extract insights from server logs for monitoring and security.

7.2 Using LangGraph to Build a Multi-Step Pipeline

Extracting information from documents is only the first step in an **AI-powered document processing workflow**. The next challenge is to **process, analyze, and structure** the extracted text in an efficient and scalable way. This is where **LangGraph**, a graph-based execution framework for LangChain, becomes invaluable.

This chapter introduces **LangGraph** and demonstrates how to build a **multi-step AI pipeline** for document processing. The goal is to develop an intelligent system that takes **raw extracted text** and transforms it into structured, actionable insights.

Introduction to LangGraph

Why Use a Graph-Based Execution Model?

Traditional AI workflows often rely on **linear pipelines**, where data flows sequentially through a predefined set of steps. While effective for simple tasks, this approach **lacks flexibility** and **scalability** when dealing with complex AI workflows that require conditional logic, parallel execution, and feedback loops.

LangGraph enables:

- **Flexible execution paths** – Handle branching logic dynamically.
- **Parallel processing** – Run multiple steps concurrently to optimize performance.
- **Stateful workflows** – Maintain context across different processing stages.
- **AI-driven decision-making** – Adapt execution paths based on intermediate results.

How LangGraph Works

LangGraph models an AI pipeline as a **directed graph**, where:

- **Nodes represent processing steps** (e.g., text cleaning, entity extraction).

- **Edges define the execution flow** (e.g., passing cleaned text to summarization).
- **State management** ensures data persistence across steps.

Designing a Multi-Step Document Processing Pipeline

A **document processing AI pipeline** typically involves the following steps:

1. **Text Ingestion** – Accept extracted text from PDFs or TXT files.
2. **Preprocessing** – Clean and normalize text for consistency.
3. **Named Entity Recognition (NER)** – Extract structured entities (e.g., names, dates, locations).
4. **Summarization** – Generate concise summaries of large documents.
5. **Embedding & Storage** – Convert text into vector embeddings for AI-driven search and retrieval.
6. **User Query Handling** – Answer questions based on processed documents.

Implementing the Pipeline with LangGraph

1. Installing Required Dependencies

Ensure that the necessary libraries are installed:

bash

```
pip install langchain langgraph openai
```

2. Defining the Pipeline Structure

First, set up the **graph framework** and define the pipeline's execution steps.

Python

python

```
import langgraph

from langchain.schema import Document


# Initialize LangGraph

graph = langgraph.Graph()


# Define the processing steps as nodes
```

```python
def preprocess_text(text):

    """Cleans extracted text for further
processing."""

    text = text.strip().replace("\n", " ")

    return {"clean_text": text}



def extract_entities(state):

    """Extracts named entities from the
cleaned text."""

    text = state["clean_text"]

    # Simulating an entity extraction
process

    entities        =       {"organizations":
["OpenAI"], "dates": ["2025-02-11"]}

    return {"entities": entities}



def summarize_text(state):

    """Generates a summary of the
document."""
```

```python
    text = state["clean_text"]

    summary = f"Summary of document:
{text[:100]}..."  # Placeholder summary

    return {"summary": summary}


# Add nodes to the graph

graph.add_node("preprocess",
preprocess_text)

graph.add_node("extract_entities",
extract_entities)

graph.add_node("summarize",
summarize_text)


# Define execution flow

graph.add_edge("preprocess",
"extract_entities")

graph.add_edge("preprocess", "summarize")

# Set the starting node

graph.set_entry_point("preprocess")
```

Breakdown:

- **Each function represents a node in the graph.**
- **Nodes execute in parallel** (both entity extraction and summarization process cleaned text).
- **State persists across nodes**, allowing later stages to access previous results.

---

3. Running the Pipeline with Sample Text

Now, execute the graph with a **sample extracted document**.

Python

python

```
# Define input text (simulated extracted
content)

extracted_text = "OpenAI was founded on
December 11, 2015, to promote and develop
friendly AI."

# Run the pipeline

state          =          graph.run({"text":
extracted_text})
```

```
# Display results

print("Entities                  Extracted:",
state["entities"])

print("Document                    Summary:",
state["summary"])
```

Expected Output:

csharp

```
Entities    Extracted:    {'organizations':
['OpenAI'], 'dates': ['2025-02-11']}

Document  Summary:  Summary  of  document:
OpenAI was founded on December 11, 2015, to
promote and develop friendly AI....
```

Enhancing the Pipeline with AI Models

Integrating a Language Model for Named Entity Recognition (NER)

Instead of manually extracting entities, we can use **OpenAI's GPT model** for improved accuracy.

Python

python

```python
from langchain.chat_models import ChatOpenAI

from langchain.schema import SystemMessage, HumanMessage

# Initialize OpenAI model

llm = ChatOpenAI(model="gpt-4", temperature=0)


def extract_entities_with_ai(state):
    """Uses an AI model to extract named entities from text."""

    text = state["clean_text"]


    messages = [

        SystemMessage(content="Extract named entities (organizations, dates, locations) from the given text."),
```

```python
        HumanMessage(content=text)

    ]


    response = llm(messages)

    return {"entities": response.content}


# Replace the manual entity extraction node
with AI-powered extraction

graph.add_node("extract_entities",
extract_entities_with_ai)
```

Now, entity extraction is **AI-powered**, providing more accurate and contextual results.

Adding Vector Storage for Search and Retrieval

To enable **semantic search** across processed documents, store extracted text as **embeddings** in a vector database like **FAISS** or **Weaviate**.

Python

python

```python
from langchain.vectorstores import FAISS

from langchain.embeddings.openai import OpenAIEmbeddings


# Initialize vector store

vectorstore = FAISS(OpenAIEmbeddings())

def store_embeddings(state):

    """Converts text into vector embeddings and stores them."""

    text = state["clean_text"]

    doc = Document(page_content=text)

    vectorstore.add_documents([doc])

    return {"embedding_stored": True}


# Add embedding storage as a pipeline step

graph.add_node("store_embeddings",
store_embeddings)
```

```
graph.add_edge("preprocess",
"store_embeddings")
```

With this enhancement, **documents can now be queried using AI-driven semantic search**.

Real-World Applications of LangGraph AI Pipelines

1. Automated Contract Analysis

- Extract key clauses, parties, and dates from contracts.
- Summarize contract terms for quick review.

2. Financial Document Processing

- Analyze invoices and extract financial details.
- Automate credit risk assessment based on extracted insights.

3. AI-Powered Knowledge Management

- Convert corporate documents into searchable knowledge bases.
- Enable intelligent Q&A over company policies.

4. Healthcare Document Processing

- Extract patient details and treatment plans from medical reports.
- Summarize research papers for medical professionals.

7.3 Deploying and Optimizing Performance

Once an AI pipeline is developed using **LangGraph and LangChain**, the next critical step is **deployment and optimization**. Deploying a multi-step AI pipeline in production involves considerations such as **scalability, latency, fault tolerance, and resource efficiency**.

This chapter provides a **comprehensive guide** on:

- **Deploying LangGraph pipelines** in cloud and containerized environments.
- **Optimizing performance** for real-time and batch processing.
- **Monitoring, debugging, and scaling AI workflows.**

By the end of this chapter, readers will have a **production-ready approach** to deploying LangGraph-based AI pipelines efficiently.

---

1. Deployment Strategies for AI Pipelines

Deploying an AI pipeline involves making the system **accessible, scalable, and reliable**. Several deployment models can be used based on use case requirements:

1.1. Deployment Models

Model	Use Case	Pros	Cons
Local Deployment	Prototyping, development, testing	Easy setup, no cloud dependency	Limited scalability, requires manual execution
Server Deployment	Small-scale production pipelines	Dedicated server, more control	Requires maintenance, single point of failure
Containerized (Docker, Kubernetes)	Scalable cloud deployment	Portable, scalable, infrastructure-agnostic	Requires container orchestration knowledge

Serverless (AWS Lambda, Google Cloud Functions)	Event-driven tasks	Cost-effective, auto-scaling	Limited execution time, cold start latency
Microservices (FastAPI, Flask, gRPC)	API-driven pipelines	Modular, scalable, supports multiple clients	Requires service orchestration (e.g., Kubernetes)

For **scalable and flexible deployment**, a **containerized microservices approach** using **Docker, Kubernetes, and FastAPI** is recommended.

---

2. Deploying LangGraph Pipelines with FastAPI and Docker

2.1. Creating an API for LangGraph Pipelines

To make the LangGraph pipeline accessible to external applications, wrap it in a **FastAPI-based web service**.

Python

```python
from fastapi import FastAPI

from pydantic import BaseModel

import langgraph

# Define API

app = FastAPI()

# Input schema

class InputData(BaseModel):
    text: str


# Initialize LangGraph pipeline

graph = langgraph.Graph()


def preprocess_text(text):
    """Preprocesses    text    before    AI
processing."""

    return                    {"clean_text":
text.strip().replace("\n", " ")}
```

```python
def summarize_text(state):

    """Summarizes the input text."""

    summary = f"Summary: {state['clean_text'][:100]}..."

    return {"summary": summary}


# Define LangGraph pipeline nodes

graph.add_node("preprocess", preprocess_text)

graph.add_node("summarize", summarize_text)

graph.add_edge("preprocess", "summarize")

graph.set_entry_point("preprocess")


@app.post("/process_text/")

def process_text(data: InputData):
```

```python
    """Processes text using the LangGraph
pipeline."""

    result        =        graph.run({"text":
data.text})

    return {"summary": result["summary"]}



# Run with: uvicorn filename:app --host
0.0.0.0 --port 8000
```

Breakdown:

- **FastAPI** provides a lightweight API wrapper around the LangGraph pipeline.
- **Pydantic** ensures structured input validation.
- **Uvicorn** serves the API efficiently.

2.2. Containerizing with Docker

Create a `Dockerfile` to containerize the FastAPI service:

dockerfile

```dockerfile
FROM python:3.10

WORKDIR /app
```

```
COPY requirements.txt .

RUN pip install -r requirements.txt

COPY . .

CMD ["uvicorn", "main:app", "--host",
"0.0.0.0", "--port", "8000"]
```

Build and run the container:

bash

```
docker build -t langgraph-api .

docker run -p 8000:8000 langgraph-api
```

Now, the **AI pipeline is accessible via an API**, ready to integrate into applications.

---

3. Optimizing Performance for AI Pipelines

3.1. Latency Optimization

Reducing **processing time** is crucial for real-time AI applications.

Techniques to Reduce Latency

- **Parallel Execution:** Process multiple pipeline steps simultaneously.
- **Batch Processing:** Group multiple inputs to reduce API calls.
- **Model Quantization:** Reduce AI model size for faster inference.
- **Efficient Caching:** Cache intermediate results to avoid redundant computation.

Example: Running multiple AI tasks in parallel using concurrent futures

python

```python
import concurrent.futures

def process_text(text):

    """Simulated          text          processing
function."""

    return text.upper()



texts  =  ["Document  1",  "Document  2",
"Document 3"]

# Parallel execution
```

```
with
concurrent.futures.ThreadPoolExecutor() as
executor:

    results                              =
list(executor.map(process_text, texts))


print(results)
```

3.2. Scaling AI Pipelines

As workloads increase, **horizontal scaling** (adding more instances) and **vertical scaling** (improving hardware) become essential.

Scaling Techniques

- **Kubernetes Autoscaling:** Automatically scales based on demand.
- **Load Balancers:** Distributes traffic across multiple pipeline instances.
- **Serverless Functions:** Dynamically allocate resources per request.

Example: Kubernetes Deployment for LangGraph API
Create a deployment.yaml file:

yaml

```yaml
apiVersion: apps/v1

kind: Deployment

metadata:

  name: langgraph-api

spec:

  replicas: 3

  selector:

    matchLabels:

      app: langgraph

  template:

    metadata:

      labels:

        app: langgraph

    spec:

      containers:

      - name: langgraph
```

```
image: langgraph-api:latest

ports:

- containerPort: 8000
```

Apply deployment:

bash

```
kubectl apply -f deployment.yaml
```

---

4. Monitoring and Debugging AI Pipelines

4.1. Logging with Prometheus and Grafana

- Use **Prometheus** for real-time metrics collection.
- Use **Grafana** to visualize pipeline performance.

4.2. Distributed Tracing with OpenTelemetry

- Tracks AI pipeline execution across multiple components.
- Helps debug bottlenecks in complex workflows.

Example: Adding OpenTelemetry to FastAPI Service

python

```python
from opentelemetry.instrumentation.fastapi
import FastAPIInstrumentor

app = FastAPI()

FastAPIInstrumentor.instrument_app(app)
```

---

5. Common Pitfalls and How to Avoid Them

5.1. API Bottlenecks

- **Use async processing** to prevent blocking API calls.

5.2. High Latency in AI Model Execution

- **Optimize model inference with TensorRT or ONNX.**

5.3. Data Storage Inefficiencies

- **Use vector databases like FAISS for fast semantic search.**

---

6. Real-World Applications of Optimized AI Pipelines

6.1. AI-Powered Customer Support

- Deploy a chatbot with LangGraph to handle user queries efficiently.

6.2. Financial Document Processing

- Scale document ingestion and analysis for large datasets.

6.3. Real-Time News Summarization

- Process and summarize news articles with low-latency AI models.

Chapter 8: Project 2 – AI-Powered Customer Support Chatbot

In this chapter, we will build an AI-powered customer support chatbot using LangChain. Unlike simple rule-based chatbots, this system will handle multi-turn conversations, remember past interactions, and deploy to a web interface for real-world usability.

What You Will Learn

- Implementing a multi-turn chatbot with LangChain.
- Enhancing the chatbot with memory and context awareness.
- Deploying the chatbot as a web application using FastAPI and Streamlit.
- Optimizing performance for scalability and real-world use cases.

This project is designed to simulate an enterprise-grade customer support assistant capable of handling real-time queries efficiently.

8.1 Implementing a Multi-Turn Chatbot with LangChain

Building an AI-powered chatbot that can engage in meaningful, multi-turn conversations is essential for real-world applications such as customer support, virtual assistants, and automated query resolution. Unlike basic rule-based chatbots that rely on predefined responses, multi-turn chatbots leverage large language models (LLMs) to generate dynamic and context-aware responses.

In this section, we will implement a multi-turn chatbot using **LangChain**, an AI framework designed for building language model-powered applications. This chatbot will:

- Maintain conversation flow across multiple turns.
- Generate coherent responses using an LLM.
- Support dynamic conversations rather than isolated responses.

By the end of this chapter, you will have a fully functional chatbot that can be expanded with memory, context awareness, and deployment in later sections.

Understanding Multi-Turn Conversations

A **multi-turn chatbot** enables users to have an ongoing conversation where each response considers prior messages. This requires:

1. **Processing sequential user inputs.**
2. **Maintaining conversation history.**
3. **Generating responses based on context rather than isolated queries.**

For example, in a customer support scenario:

- **User:** "I need help with my order."
- **Bot:** "Sure, could you provide your order number?"
- **User:** "It's 12345."
- **Bot:** "Thank you. Your order is scheduled for delivery tomorrow."

A basic chatbot without context would not remember the order number from the previous message, making conversations inefficient. To handle this, we need **conversation chains** that retain context throughout an interaction.

Setting Up the Development Environment

To build our chatbot, we will use LangChain along with OpenAI's GPT model for response generation.

Step 1: Installing Dependencies

Ensure you have Python installed, then install the necessary packages:

bash

```
pip install langchain openai
```

You will also need an OpenAI API key to use GPT models. Set it as an environment variable:

bash

```
export OPENAI_API_KEY="your-api-key-here"
```

Alternatively, you can specify the key directly in code, but it's recommended to store it securely.

Building the Multi-Turn Chatbot Core

Now, let's create a chatbot using **LangChain's ConversationChain**, which enables contextual conversation handling.

Step 1: Importing Required Modules

Python:

python

```
from langchain.llms import OpenAI

from langchain.chains import ConversationChain
```

Step 2: Creating the Chatbot Class

We will define a chatbot that uses an LLM to process conversations.

Python:

python

```python
class MultiTurnChatbot:

    def __init__(self, model_name="gpt-4"):

        """Initializes the chatbot with a language model."""

        self.llm = OpenAI(model_name=model_name)

        self.conversation = ConversationChain(llm=self.llm)


    def get_response(self, user_input):

        """Processes user input and returns an AI-generated response."""
```

```python
    return
self.conversation.run(user_input)
```

This class initializes an **LLM** and a **conversation chain**, ensuring responses consider past interactions.

Testing the Chatbot

To verify that our chatbot functions correctly, we can create an instance and test interactions.

Python:

python

```python
if __name__ == "__main__":

    bot = MultiTurnChatbot()

    while True:

        user_query = input("User: ")

        if user_query.lower() == "exit":

            break
```

```
        response                                  =
bot.get_response(user_query)

        print("Bot:", response)
```

Expected Behavior:

1. The chatbot receives user input.
2. The **ConversationChain** processes it using GPT.
3. A coherent response is generated, considering past messages.

This chatbot already supports **multi-turn conversations**, but its memory is limited to the session. To enhance user experience, we will integrate **long-term memory** in the next section.

Common Pitfalls and Solutions

Issue	Possible Cause	Solution
Chatbot forgets context	No memory persistence	Use memory modules (covered in the next section)

Repetitive or generic responses	Low model temperature	Increase temperature parameter in `OpenAI()`
API rate limits	Exceeding OpenAI limits	Implement rate limiting or caching
Poor response quality	Inadequate prompt tuning	Modify conversation prompts for better clarity

These pitfalls are common in AI chatbot development, but LangChain provides solutions that we will explore in the following sections.

Next Steps

Now that we have implemented a functional multi-turn chatbot, we will improve it by adding **memory and context awareness** in the next chapter. This enhancement will allow our chatbot to remember user-specific details, improving its conversational flow and usability.

8.2 Adding Memory and Context Awareness

A truly effective AI chatbot must go beyond responding to isolated user queries. It should be capable of **remembering past interactions**, maintaining **context**, and adapting responses based on prior conversations. This is especially important in applications like customer support, where users expect continuity in discussions.

In this chapter, we will enhance our chatbot from the previous section by integrating **memory and context awareness** using **LangChain's memory modules**. By the end of this chapter, our chatbot will:

- Maintain conversational history across interactions.
- Store and retrieve relevant user details dynamically.
- Improve engagement by generating context-aware responses.

This section will cover different types of memory in LangChain, practical implementations, and best practices for managing conversation state efficiently.

Understanding Memory in LangChain

Memory in LangChain enables chatbots to recall user inputs across multiple turns. Unlike stateless models that treat every query as new, a memory-enabled chatbot can maintain history, making conversations more natural and useful.

Types of Memory in LangChain

LangChain provides several memory implementations:

Memory Type	Description	Use Case
ConversationBuffer Memory	Stores raw conversation history as a list of messages.	Suitable for short conversations with minimal storage overhead.
ConversationSumma ryMemory	Uses an LLM to summarize past interactions into key points.	Ideal for long conversations where storing full history is inefficient.

ConversationBuffer WindowMemory	Keeps only the most recent messages in history.	Useful for applications requiring limited context retention.
ConversationEntity Memory	Tracks specific entities (e.g., user names, preferences).	Great for customer support and personalized experiences.

We will explore and implement **ConversationBufferMemory** first, then discuss **advanced memory techniques**.

Integrating Memory into the Chatbot

To enable memory in our chatbot, we modify the existing **ConversationChain** to include a memory component.

Step 1: Installing Dependencies

Ensure you have LangChain installed:

bash

```
pip install langchain openai
```

Step 2: Updating the Chatbot to Use Memory

We will modify our chatbot to use **ConversationBufferMemory**, which stores past interactions.

Python:

python

```python
from langchain.llms import OpenAI

from langchain.chains import ConversationChain

from langchain.memory import ConversationBufferMemory


class MemoryChatbot:
    def __init__(self, model_name="gpt-4"):
        """Initializes chatbot with memory-enabled conversation chain."""
        self.llm = OpenAI(model_name=model_name)
```

```python
        self.memory                          =
ConversationBufferMemory()       #   Enables
conversation history tracking

        self.conversation                    =
ConversationChain(llm=self.llm,
memory=self.memory)



    def get_response(self, user_input):

        """Processes user input and returns
an AI-generated response with memory."""

        return
self.conversation.run(user_input)
```

Step 3: Testing Context Retention

Now, let's test whether the chatbot remembers previous interactions.

Python:

python

```python
if __name__ == "__main__":
```

```python
bot = MemoryChatbot()

print("Chatbot    initialized.    Type
'exit' to end conversation.")

while True:

    user_query = input("User: ")

    if user_query.lower() == "exit":

        break

    response                        =
bot.get_response(user_query)

    print("Bot:", response)
```

Expected Behavior:

Without Memory:

- **User:** "I need help with my order."
- **Bot:** "Can you provide more details?"
- **User:** "My order number is 12345."
- **Bot:** "I'm sorry, I don't have that information."

With Memory:

- **User:** "I need help with my order."

- **Bot:** "Can you provide more details?"
- **User:** "My order number is 12345."
- **Bot:** "Thank you! Your order is scheduled for delivery tomorrow."

This demonstrates how the chatbot **remembers prior exchanges**, making conversations more seamless.

Advanced Memory Techniques

Using ConversationSummaryMemory

If a chatbot handles long interactions, storing raw messages becomes inefficient. Instead, **ConversationSummaryMemory** compresses past exchanges into a **concise summary**, allowing the model to process key points without unnecessary details.

Implementation:

Python:

python

```
from          langchain.memory          import
ConversationSummaryMemory

class SummaryMemoryChatbot:
```

```python
    def __init__(self, model_name="gpt-4"):

        """Initializes chatbot with summarized memory."""

        self.llm = OpenAI(model_name=model_name)

        self.memory = ConversationSummaryMemory(llm=self.llm)

        self.conversation = ConversationChain(llm=self.llm,
        memory=self.memory)

    def get_response(self, user_input):

        """Generates responses while maintaining summarized conversation history."""

        return self.conversation.run(user_input)
```

Using Entity-Based Memory

For personalized interactions, **ConversationEntityMemory** tracks specific user details (e.g., name, preferences). This is particularly useful in customer support applications where users expect personalized responses.

Implementation:

Python:

python

```
from         langchain.memory         import
ConversationEntityMemory

class EntityMemoryChatbot:

    def   __init__(self,   model_name="gpt-
4"):

        """"Initializes      chatbot      with
entity-aware memory."""

        self.llm                          =
OpenAI(model_name=model_name)

        self.memory                       =
ConversationEntityMemory(llm=self.llm)
```

```
        self.conversation            =
ConversationChain(llm=self.llm,
memory=self.memory)

    def get_response(self, user_input):

        """Generates      responses      while
remembering user-specific details."""

        return
self.conversation.run(user_input)
```

This enables interactions like:

- **User:** "My name is Alex."
- **Bot:** "Nice to meet you, Alex! How can I assist you today?"
- **User:** "What's my name?"
- **Bot:** "Your name is Alex."

Choosing the Right Memory Strategy

When designing an AI chatbot, selecting the right memory module depends on the use case:

Scenario	Recommended Memory Type
Short conversations (FAQ bots)	ConversationBufferMemory
Long discussions (support tickets)	ConversationSummaryMemory
Keeping track of recent messages only	ConversationBufferWindowMemory
Personalization (customer support)	ConversationEntityMemory

A hybrid approach is often best—combining entity memory for user details with buffer or summary memory for past messages.

Common Pitfalls and Solutions

Issue	Cause	Solution
Chatbot forgets old messages	Memory is too short	Use ConversationSummaryMemory
Responses become repetitive	LLM lacks varied context	Tune prompt engineering and memory refresh
API cost increases	Too much context sent in API calls	Use summarized memory instead of full history
Privacy concerns	Storing sensitive user data	Implement encryption and compliance measures

These issues are common in AI chatbot development, but selecting the right memory management strategy helps mitigate them.

8.3 Deploying the Chatbot to a Web Interface

After building a multi-turn chatbot with **memory and context awareness**, the next step is to deploy it as a **web application**. Deployment is crucial for integrating the chatbot into real-world applications, enabling users to interact with it via a browser or mobile device.

In this chapter, we will:

- Set up a **FastAPI** backend for the chatbot.
- Create a **React-based frontend** to provide a user-friendly interface.
- Integrate the backend and frontend for a seamless chatbot experience.
- Deploy the chatbot to a **cloud platform** (e.g., AWS, Render, or Vercel).

By the end, you will have a **fully functional, web-accessible AI-powered chatbot** built with **LangChain and LangGraph**.

Choosing the Right Deployment Stack

Deploying an AI chatbot requires both a **backend** (to process queries) and a **frontend** (to display responses). Here's a breakdown of the stack we'll use:

Component	Technology	Purpose
Backend API	FastAPI	Handles chatbot requests
AI Processing	LangChain + OpenAI	Generates chatbot responses
Frontend UI	React + Vite	Provides a chat interface
Database (Optional)	Redis/PostgreSQL	Stores conversation history
Deployment	AWS, Render, Vercel	Hosts the chatbot

This stack ensures a **fast, scalable, and user-friendly** chatbot deployment.

Step 1: Setting Up the FastAPI Backend

The backend will serve as the chatbot's API, receiving user messages and returning responses.

Installing Dependencies

First, install the required Python packages:

bash

```bash
pip install fastapi uvicorn langchain openai pydantic
```

Creating the API Server

Create a file called `main.py` and add the following FastAPI code:

Python (`main.py`):

python

```python
from fastapi import FastAPI

from pydantic import BaseModel
```

```python
from langchain.llms import OpenAI

from langchain.chains import import
ConversationChain

from langchain.memory import
ConversationBufferMemory

import os

# Initialize FastAPI app

app = FastAPI()

# Load OpenAI API key

os.environ["OPENAI_API_KEY"] = "your-api-
key"

# Initialize chatbot with memory

llm = OpenAI(model_name="gpt-4")

memory = ConversationBufferMemory()

conversation = ConversationChain(llm=llm,
memory=memory)

# Define request model

class ChatRequest(BaseModel):
```

```python
    user_input: str

@app.post("/chat/")

async     def     chat_endpoint(request:
ChatRequest):

    """Handles chatbot interactions."""

    response                                  =
conversation.run(request.user_input)

    return {"response": response}
```

Running the API Server

Start the FastAPI server:

bash

```bash
uvicorn main:app --host 0.0.0.0 --port 8000
--reload
```

Once running, visit `http://localhost:8000/docs` to test the API using FastAPI's interactive documentation.

Step 2: Building the Frontend with React and Vite

To provide a user-friendly chat interface, we'll use **React with Vite**.

Setting Up the React Project

Run the following commands to create and set up a React project:

bash

```
npm create vite@latest chatbot-ui --template react

cd chatbot-ui

npm install

npm install axios
```

Creating the Chat Interface

Replace the contents of src/App.jsx with the following code:

JavaScript (App.jsx):

javascript

```
import React, { useState } from "react";
```

269

```javascript
import axios from "axios";

function App() {

    const [messages, setMessages] =
useState([]);

    const [input, setInput] = useState("");

    const sendMessage = async () => {

        if (!input.trim()) return;

        const userMessage = { text: input,
sender: "User" };

        setMessages([...messages,
userMessage]);

        try {

            const response = await
axios.post("http://localhost:8000/chat/",
{

                user_input: input,

            });
```

```
            const botMessage = { text:
response.data.response, sender: "Bot" };

            setMessages([...messages,
userMessage, botMessage]);

        } catch (error) {

            console.error("Error  fetching
response:", error);

        }

        setInput("");

    };

    return (

        <div className="chat-container">

            <div className="chat-box">

                {messages.map((msg,  index)
=> (

                    <div        key={index}
className={`message ${msg.sender}`}>

                        {msg.text}

                    </div>
```

```jsx
          ))}

        </div>

        <input

            type="text"

            value={input}

            onChange={(e)              =>
setInput(e.target.value)}

            placeholder="Type            a
message..."

          />

          <button
onClick={sendMessage}>Send</button>

      </div>

    );

}

export default App;
```

Styling the Chat Interface

Replace src/index.css with:

CSS (index.css):

css

```css
.chat-container {

    width: 400px;

    margin: auto;

    border: 1px solid #ccc;

    padding: 20px;

    background-color: #f9f9f9;

}

.chat-box {

    height: 300px;

    overflow-y: auto;

    margin-bottom: 10px;

}

.message {
```

```css
    padding: 8px;

    border-radius: 5px;

    margin: 5px 0;

}

.User {

    text-align: right;

    background-color: #dcf8c6;

}

.Bot {

    text-align: left;

    background-color: #e8e8e8;

}
```

Running the Frontend

Start the React app:

bash

```bash
npm run dev
```

Now, visit `http://localhost:5173` in your browser to test the chatbot.

Step 3: Connecting the Backend and Frontend

Modify the API URL in `App.jsx` to match your backend's deployment URL when going live:

javascript

```javascript
const         response         =         await
axios.post("https://your-backend-
url/chat/", {

    user_input: input,

});
```

Step 4: Deploying the Chatbot

Now that we have a working chatbot, let's deploy it.

Deploying the Backend

Option 1: Deploy on Render

1. Push the FastAPI code to GitHub.

2. Create a **Render** account and select "New Web Service."
3. Connect your GitHub repository and choose **FastAPI**.

Set the **start command** as:
bash

```
uvicorn main:app --host 0.0.0.0 --port $PORT
```

4. Deploy and copy the API URL.

Option 2: Deploy on AWS Lambda (Optional)

Use `serverless-fastapi` for a lightweight deployment.

bash

```
pip install mangum
```

Modify `main.py`:

python

```
from mangum import Mangum

handler = Mangum(app)
```

Deploying the Frontend

Option 1: Deploy on Vercel

1. Push the React app to GitHub.

Install Vercel CLI:
bash
```
npm install -g vercel
```

Deploy:
bash
```
vercel
```

Option 2: Deploy on Netlify

1. Push the React app to GitHub.
2. Connect GitHub repo to Netlify and deploy.

Chapter 9: Project 3 – Intelligent Data Analysis Workflow

Data analysis is at the core of decision-making in modern enterprises. With the rise of **AI-driven analytics**, businesses can automate insights generation, forecast trends, and generate reports without manual intervention. This chapter will guide you through building an **Intelligent Data Analysis Workflow** using **LangGraph and LangChain**, integrating AI models for predictions, and automating reporting and alerts.

By the end of this chapter, you will have a production-ready AI pipeline that:

1. **Ingests and preprocesses raw data** automatically.
2. **Extracts key insights** using LangGraph's workflow orchestration.
3. **Uses AI models for predictive analysis.**
4. **Generates automated reports and real-time alerts.**

This project will demonstrate **end-to-end AI-powered data intelligence**, helping businesses make data-driven decisions with minimal manual intervention.

9.1 Using LangGraph for Automated Data Insights

In data-driven applications, the ability to automatically generate insights from structured and unstructured data is critical. Traditional data pipelines require significant manual effort to preprocess, analyze, and extract key insights. However, **LangGraph**, a powerful framework for orchestrating AI workflows, enables developers to automate this process efficiently.

This chapter explores how to use **LangGraph** to build an **automated data analysis workflow**. We will cover:

1. **Understanding LangGraph's graph-based architecture** for AI-driven data workflows.
2. **Setting up a data pipeline** for ingestion, cleaning, and preprocessing.
3. **Integrating an LLM** for automatic insight generation.
4. **Structuring relationships in data** using a knowledge graph.
5. **Generating visualizations and reports** to aid decision-making.

By the end of this chapter, you will have a fully functional **AI-powered data analytics pipeline**, capable of extracting meaningful insights from raw data with minimal manual intervention.

Understanding LangGraph for AI-Driven Workflows

LangGraph extends **LangChain** by introducing a **graph-based execution model**. Unlike sequential pipelines, which process data linearly, **LangGraph** enables a more **modular, scalable, and parallelizable** approach to AI workflows.

Key Features of LangGraph in Data Insights Pipelines

- **Directed Graph Execution** – Define a structured flow of operations.
- **Parallel Processing** – Execute multiple AI components simultaneously.
- **State Management** – Maintain memory across workflow steps.
- **Event-Driven Processing** – Automate decision-making based on AI-generated insights.

How It Fits into Data Insights

A LangGraph-based AI workflow for data insights typically involves:

1. **Data ingestion and preprocessing** (loading CSV, JSON, or API data).
2. **Feature engineering** (transforming raw data into useful attributes).

3. **AI-driven analysis** (LLMs extracting key insights).
4. **Knowledge structuring** (organizing insights into a graph-based representation).
5. **Automated reporting and alerting** (delivering insights to end-users).

Building an Automated Data Insights Workflow

We will now build a **LangGraph-powered AI workflow** that ingests data, extracts insights using an LLM, and structures them into a knowledge graph.

Step 1: Install Dependencies

Before we begin, install the required libraries:

bash

```
pip install langchain langgraph pandas openai networkx matplotlib seaborn
```

Step 2: Defining the LangGraph Workflow

Our AI-driven data insights pipeline consists of the following **graph nodes**:

- **Ingestion Node** – Loads raw data.
- **Preprocessing Node** – Cleans and transforms data.
- **Insight Generation Node** – Uses an LLM to extract insights.
- **Graph Construction Node** – Converts data into a structured knowledge graph.
- **Visualization Node** – Generates graphical reports.

We define the workflow in **LangGraph** below:

Python (data_workflow.py)

python

```
import pandas as pd

import langgraph

from     langchain.chat_models     import
ChatOpenAI

from     langchain.prompts     import
PromptTemplate

import networkx as nx

import matplotlib.pyplot as plt


# Load AI model
```

```python
llm = ChatOpenAI(model_name="gpt-4")


# Step 1: Load data

def load_data():

    df = pd.read_csv("data.csv")  # Replace
with real data source

    return df


# Step 2: Preprocess data

def preprocess_data(df):

    df = df.dropna()   # Remove missing
values

    df.columns                         =
[col.strip().lower().replace(" ", "_") for
col in df.columns]   # Normalize column
names

    return df


# Step 3: Generate insights using LLM
```

```python
def generate_insights(df):

    data_sample = df.head(10).to_string()

    prompt = f"Analyze the following
dataset and summarize key
insights:\n\n{data_sample}"

    response = llm.predict(prompt)

    return response



# Step 4: Construct a knowledge graph

def build_knowledge_graph(insights):

    G = nx.Graph()

    for i, insight in
enumerate(insights.split(". ")):

        G.add_node(f"Insight {i+1}",
text=insight)

    return G



# Step 5: Generate a visualization
```

```python
def visualize_graph(G):

    pos = nx.spring_layout(G)

    labels  =  nx.get_node_attributes(G,
'text')

    nx.draw(G,   pos,   with_labels=True,
node_size=3000, node_color="lightblue")

    nx.draw_networkx_labels(G,       pos,
labels, font_size=8)

    plt.title("Knowledge     Graph     of
Insights")

    plt.show()

# Define LangGraph nodes

workflow = langgraph.Graph()

workflow.add_node("Load Data", load_data)

workflow.add_node("Preprocess       Data",
preprocess_data)

workflow.add_node("Generate    Insights",
generate_insights)
```

```python
workflow.add_node("Build Knowledge Graph",
build_knowledge_graph)

workflow.add_node("Visualize    Insights",
visualize_graph)


# Define execution order

workflow.add_edge("Load Data", "Preprocess
Data")

workflow.add_edge("Preprocess        Data",
"Generate Insights")

workflow.add_edge("Generate    Insights",
"Build Knowledge Graph")

workflow.add_edge("Build Knowledge Graph",
"Visualize Insights")


# Execute workflow

if __name__ == "__main__":

    output = workflow.run("Load Data")
```

Step 3: Running the Workflow

To execute the full data insights pipeline, run:

bash

```
python data_workflow.py
```

This will:

1. **Load the dataset** from `data.csv`.
2. **Preprocess the data** (cleaning, missing value handling).
3. **Use GPT-4 to generate insights** from the dataset.
4. **Build a knowledge graph** from extracted insights.
5. **Visualize the insights graphically** for better interpretation.

Enhancing the Workflow

1. Adding Real-Time Data Processing

Instead of loading data from CSV, integrate an **API-based data source** for real-time analysis:

python

```python
import requests

def fetch_live_data(api_url):

    response = requests.get(api_url)

    return pd.DataFrame(response.json())
```

---

2. Implementing Anomaly Detection

Automatically detect anomalies and flag alerts:

python

```python
import numpy as np

def detect_anomalies(df, column):

    mean, std = np.mean(df[column]), np.std(df[column])

    anomalies = df[np.abs(df[column] - mean) > 2 * std]

    return anomalies
```

3. Automating Reports

Automatically email reports with the extracted insights:

python

```
import smtplib

from email.message import EmailMessage

def send_email_report(insights):

    msg = EmailMessage()

    msg.set_content(insights)

    msg["Subject"]  =  "Automated  Data
Insights Report"

    msg["From"] = "your-email@example.com"

    msg["To"] = "recipient@example.com"


    with  smtplib.SMTP("smtp.example.com",
587) as server:

        server.starttls()
```

```
server.login("your-
email@example.com", "your-password")

server.send_message(msg)
```

9.2 Integrating AI Models for Predictions

Predictive analytics is at the core of AI-driven decision-making, enabling businesses to anticipate trends, detect patterns, and make informed choices. In this chapter, we will explore how to integrate **machine learning (ML) models and large language models (LLMs) into a LangGraph workflow** to create an **automated prediction system**.

This chapter will cover:

1. **Understanding predictive AI models** and their integration into LangGraph.
2. **Using LangGraph to orchestrate AI-powered predictions** efficiently.
3. **Implementing ML models (regression/classification) within LangGraph.**
4. **Leveraging LLMs for contextual and unstructured data predictions.**
5. **Deploying the AI pipeline for real-world applications.**

By the end of this chapter, you will have a **fully functional AI-powered prediction system**, capable of **handling structured and unstructured data for forecasting and decision-making.**

Understanding Predictive AI Models in LangGraph

Predictive models fall into two categories:

- **Traditional ML models** – Used for structured data predictions (e.g., sales forecasting, anomaly detection).
- **LLM-based predictions** – Used for unstructured data insights (e.g., text classification, sentiment analysis).

LangGraph allows developers to build **modular, scalable AI workflows** by integrating both traditional ML models and LLMs into a **single graph-based pipeline.**

Why Use LangGraph for AI Predictions?

- **Scalability** – Handle multiple AI models in parallel.
- **Flexibility** – Combine structured ML models with LLMs.
- **Automated Workflow** – Define dynamic paths based on AI-generated insights.
- **Stateful Execution** – Maintain data context across multiple predictions.

Building an AI-Powered Prediction Workflow

We will build a **LangGraph-based AI workflow** that:

1. **Ingests and preprocesses data** for prediction.
2. **Uses a machine learning model for structured data forecasting.**
3. **Leverages an LLM for unstructured text analysis.**
4. **Automates prediction-based decision-making.**

Step 1: Install Dependencies

Ensure all required libraries are installed:

bash

```
pip install langchain langgraph pandas
scikit-learn openai numpy networkx
matplotlib seaborn
```

Step 2: Defining the LangGraph Workflow

Our AI prediction pipeline consists of the following **graph nodes**:

- **Ingestion Node** – Loads raw data from structured and unstructured sources.

- **Preprocessing Node** – Cleans and prepares data for prediction.
- **ML Model Prediction Node** – Uses a trained model for structured predictions.
- **LLM Analysis Node** – Extracts insights from unstructured data.
- **Decision Node** – Automates actions based on predictions.

Python (prediction_workflow.py)

python

```python
import pandas as pd

import langgraph

from langchain.chat_models import ChatOpenAI

from langchain.prompts import PromptTemplate

from sklearn.model_selection import train_test_split

from sklearn.ensemble import RandomForestRegressor

import numpy as np

import networkx as nx
```

```python
import matplotlib.pyplot as plt


# Load AI model

llm = ChatOpenAI(model_name="gpt-4")

# Step 1: Load data

def load_data():

    df = pd.read_csv("data.csv")  # Replace
with actual dataset

    return df


# Step 2: Preprocess data

def preprocess_data(df):

    df = df.dropna()

    df.columns                          =
[col.strip().lower().replace(" ", "_") for
col in df.columns]

    return df
```

```python
# Step 3: Train ML model for structured
predictions

def train_ml_model(df):

    X = df.drop(columns=["target"])

    y = df["target"]


    X train,  X test,  y train,  y test  =
train_test_split(X,    y,    test_size=0.2,
random_state=42)

    model                               =
RandomForestRegressor(n_estimators=100,
random_state=42)

    model.fit(X_train, y_train)


    return model


# Step 4: Predict with ML model

def predict_with_ml(model, df):

    X = df.drop(columns=["target"])
```

```python
    predictions = model.predict(X)

    df["prediction"] = predictions

    return df


# Step 5: Generate insights using LLM

def analyze_text_with_llm(text_data):

    prompt = f"Analyze the following report
and provide insights:\n\n{text_data}"

    response = llm.predict(prompt)

    return response


# Step 6: Automate decision-making

def decision_making(predictions):

    high_risk                            =
predictions[predictions["prediction"]    >
0.8]

    if not high_risk.empty:
```

```python
        return  f"Alert:  {len(high_risk)}
high-risk cases detected."

    return "No critical alerts."


# Define LangGraph nodes

workflow = langgraph.Graph()

workflow.add_node("Load Data", load_data)

workflow.add_node("Preprocess     Data",
preprocess_data)

workflow.add_node("Train    ML    Model",
train_ml_model)

workflow.add_node("Predict   with   ML",
predict_with_ml)

workflow.add_node("Analyze Text with LLM",
analyze_text_with_llm)

workflow.add_node("Decision      Making",
decision_making)

# Define execution order
```

```
workflow.add_edge("Load Data", "Preprocess
Data")

workflow.add_edge("Preprocess        Data",
"Train ML Model")

workflow.add_edge("Train      ML      Model",
"Predict with ML")

workflow.add_edge("Predict      with      ML",
"Decision Making")

workflow.add_edge("Analyze Text with LLM",
"Decision Making")


# Execute workflow

if __name__ == "__main__":

    output = workflow.run("Load Data")

    print(output)
```

Step 3: Running the AI Prediction Pipeline

To execute the workflow, run:

bash

```bash
python prediction_workflow.py
```

This will:

1. **Load the dataset** from `data.csv`.
2. **Preprocess the data** (handling missing values, normalization).
3. **Train a machine learning model** for structured predictions.
4. **Use GPT-4 to analyze unstructured data.**
5. **Automate decision-making based on prediction results.**

Enhancing the AI Prediction Workflow

1. Integrating Real-Time Data Sources

Modify data ingestion to support API-based real-time updates:

python

```python
import requests

def fetch_live_data(api_url):
    response = requests.get(api_url)
```

```python
    return pd.DataFrame(response.json())
```

---

2. Deploying AI Models via API

Expose the prediction model as an API for external applications:

python

```python
from flask import Flask, request, jsonify

import joblib

app = Flask(__name__)

model = joblib.load("model.pkl")


@app.route('/predict', methods=['POST'])

def predict():

    data = request.get_json()

    predictions                              =
model.predict(data["features"])

    return           jsonify({"predictions":
predictions.tolist()})
```

```python
if __name__ == "__main__":

    app.run(debug=True)
```

3. Incorporating Anomaly Detection

Detect anomalies in predictions and flag critical cases:

python

```python
import numpy as np

def detect_anomalies(df, column):

    mean, std = np.mean(df[column]), np.std(df[column])

    anomalies = df[np.abs(df[column] - mean) > 2 * std]

    return anomalies
```

4. Automating Alerts and Reports

Trigger automated alerts when predictions exceed a threshold:

python

```python
import smtplib

from email.message import EmailMessage

def send_alert(message):

    msg = EmailMessage()

    msg.set_content(message)

    msg["Subject"] = "AI Prediction Alert"

    msg["From"] = "your-email@example.com"

    msg["To"] = "recipient@example.com"


    with  smtplib.SMTP("smtp.example.com",
587) as server:

        server.starttls()

        server.login("your-
email@example.com", "your-password")

        server.send_message(msg)
```

9.3 Automating Reporting and Alerts

Automated reporting and alerting play a crucial role in modern AI workflows, ensuring that stakeholders receive timely insights and notifications based on AI-generated predictions. By integrating **LangGraph with AI models, data visualization tools, and messaging systems**, we can build a fully automated reporting pipeline that delivers **customized reports, dashboards, and alerts** in real time.

In this chapter, we will cover:

1. **Understanding the importance of AI-driven reports and alerts**
2. **Designing an automated reporting pipeline with LangGraph**
3. **Generating AI-powered reports and insights using LangChain**
4. **Automating alerts via email, Slack, and real-time notifications**
5. **Deploying and scaling the system for production use**

By the end of this chapter, you will have a **functional, automated reporting and alert system**, enabling seamless integration into AI workflows for monitoring, decision-making, and business intelligence.

Understanding Automated Reporting and Alerts

Why Automate Reports and Alerts?

Manual reporting processes are slow, prone to errors, and inefficient in handling real-time insights. **Automated reporting** ensures that relevant insights are delivered without manual intervention, while **automated alerts** help detect anomalies and notify stakeholders instantly.

Key benefits:

- **Real-time insights:** Immediate access to AI-generated reports.
- **Proactive monitoring:** Automatic alerts for anomalies or critical events.
- **Scalability:** Handle large-scale data without human intervention.
- **Improved decision-making:** Timely reports help optimize strategies.

Real-World Applications

- **Financial Markets:** Detect trading anomalies and generate investment reports.
- **Healthcare:** Monitor patient data and alert medical staff to abnormalities.
- **E-commerce:** Analyze sales trends and notify about stock shortages.

- **Cybersecurity:** Identify suspicious activities and send security alerts.

Designing an Automated Reporting Pipeline with LangGraph

Our AI-powered reporting pipeline consists of the following **graph nodes**:

1. **Data Collection Node** – Fetches raw AI predictions from models.
2. **Data Processing Node** – Analyzes and summarizes insights.
3. **Report Generation Node** – Creates visualized reports using AI.
4. **Alerting Node** – Sends notifications based on predefined triggers.
5. **Delivery Node** – Distributes reports via email, Slack, or dashboards.

Workflow Overview

1. **AI predictions are generated** from ML models or LLMs.
2. **Reports are formatted with key insights and visualizations.**
3. **If anomalies are detected, alerts are triggered.**

4. **Reports and alerts are delivered automatically.**

Building the Automated Reporting System

Step 1: Install Dependencies

Ensure all required libraries are installed:

bash

```
pip install langchain langgraph pandas
matplotlib seaborn openai flask smtplib
slack_sdk
```

Step 2: Setting Up the LangGraph Workflow

We define nodes for **data ingestion, analysis, report generation, and alerting.**

Python (reporting_workflow.py)

python

```
import pandas as pd

import langgraph
```

```python
import seaborn as sns

import matplotlib.pyplot as plt

import smtplib

from email.message import EmailMessage

from slack_sdk import WebClient

from langchain.chat_models import ChatOpenAI

from langchain.prompts import PromptTemplate


# Load AI model

llm = ChatOpenAI(model_name="gpt-4")


# Slack API Configuration

slack_client = WebClient(token="your-slack-api-token")

slack_channel = "#alerts"
```

```python
# Step 1: Load AI prediction results

def load_predictions():

    df = pd.read_csv("predictions.csv")

    return df



# Step 2: Analyze data and detect anomalies

def analyze_data(df):

    threshold                              =
df["prediction"].quantile(0.95)

    anomalies  =  df[df["prediction"]  >
threshold]

    return anomalies



# Step 3: Generate AI-powered report

def generate_report(df):

    plt.figure(figsize=(8, 4))

    sns.histplot(df["prediction"],
bins=20, kde=True)
```

```python
    plt.title("Prediction Distribution")

    plt.savefig("report.png")


    summary_prompt = f"Summarize the
following AI
predictions:\n{df.head().to_string()}"

    report_summary =
llm.predict(summary_prompt)


    return f"Report
Summary:\n{report_summary}"


# Step 4: Send alerts via email

def send_email_alert(message):

    msg = EmailMessage()

    msg.set_content(message)

    msg["Subject"] = "AI Alert: Critical
Event Detected"

    msg["From"] = "your-email@example.com"
```

```python
    msg["To"] = "recipient@example.com"


    with  smtplib.SMTP("smtp.example.com",
587) as server:

        server.starttls()

        server.login("your-
email@example.com", "your-password")

        server.send_message(msg)


# Step 5: Send Slack alert

def send_slack_alert(message):


slack_client.chat_postMessage(channel=slac
k_channel, text=message)


# Define LangGraph workflow

workflow = langgraph.Graph()

workflow.add_node("Load        Predictions",
load_predictions)
```

```python
workflow.add_node("Analyze          Data",
analyze_data)

workflow.add_node("Generate          Report",
generate_report)

workflow.add_node("Send    Email    Alert",
send_email_alert)

workflow.add_node("Send    Slack    Alert",
send_slack_alert)


# Define execution order

workflow.add_edge("Load       Predictions",
"Analyze Data")

workflow.add_edge("Analyze          Data",
"Generate Report")

workflow.add_edge("Analyze   Data",   "Send
Email Alert")

workflow.add_edge("Analyze   Data",   "Send
Slack Alert")


# Execute workflow
```

```
if __name__ == "__main__":

    output       =       workflow.run("Load
Predictions")

    print(output)
```

Step 3: Running the Reporting and Alerting Pipeline

To execute the workflow, run:

bash

```
python reporting_workflow.py
```

This will:

1. **Load AI-generated predictions from a dataset.**
2. **Analyze data and identify critical anomalies.**
3. **Generate a report with AI-driven insights and visualizations.**
4. **Send alerts via email and Slack when anomalies are detected.**

Enhancing the System with Additional Features

1. Adding Real-Time Streaming with Kafka

For real-time AI reporting, integrate **Apache Kafka**:

python

```
from kafka import KafkaConsumer

def stream_data():

    consumer       =       KafkaConsumer('ai-
predictions',
bootstrap_servers='localhost:9092')

    for message in consumer:

        yield message.value
```

---

2. Storing Reports in a Dashboard (Flask API)

Expose reports as a web service using **Flask**:

python

```
from flask import Flask, send_file
```

```python
app = Flask(__name__)


@app.route('/report', methods=['GET'])

def get_report():

    return          send_file("report.png",
mimetype='image/png')



if __name__ == "__main__":

    app.run(debug=True)
```

---

3. Triggering Alerts Based on Custom Rules

Define custom rules for triggering alerts:

python

```python
def custom_alert_rules(df):

    if (df["prediction"] > 0.9).any():
```

```
        send_email_alert("Critical anomaly
detected!")

        send_slack_alert("🚨      High-risk
event detected in AI predictions!")
```

Deploying the System to Production

To **deploy** the automated reporting system:

- **Use Docker** to containerize the application.
- **Deploy on AWS Lambda** for serverless alerts.
- **Integrate with a monitoring dashboard** like Grafana.

Part 4: Ethical Considerations and Future Trends

Chapter 10: Ethical and Security Considerations in AI Workflows

As AI workflows become increasingly integral to decision-making processes, ensuring **ethical integrity and security** is paramount. AI models influence critical areas such as **healthcare, finance, hiring, law enforcement, and personalized recommendations**, making it essential to mitigate **bias, security vulnerabilities, and unintended consequences**.

This chapter will explore:

- **AI bias and fairness** – How to detect, mitigate, and prevent biased outcomes.
- **Security risks and best practices** – Strategies for safeguarding AI pipelines.
- **Responsible AI deployment** – Ensuring AI models are transparent, explainable, and aligned with ethical guidelines.

By the end of this chapter, you will have a **comprehensive understanding of AI ethics and security**, along with **practical strategies** to design robust, fair, and secure AI systems.

10.1 Addressing AI Bias and Fairness

AI models increasingly influence decision-making in critical areas such as **hiring, lending, healthcare, and law enforcement**.

However, these models are prone to bias, leading to **unfair, discriminatory, or ethically questionable outcomes**. Addressing AI bias is crucial for **ensuring fairness, trust, and regulatory compliance**.

This chapter explores:

Types of AI bias and their real-world impact. **Techniques for detecting and measuring bias** in AI workflows. **Mitigation strategies**, including data preprocessing and algorithmic fairness methods. **Implementing fairness-aware AI systems** in LangGraph and LangChain.

By the end of this chapter, you will have **practical strategies** to detect, mitigate, and prevent bias in AI models, ensuring fairness in AI-powered decision-making.

Understanding Bias in AI

AI bias occurs when a model **systematically favors or disadvantages** certain groups due to **biased data, algorithmic errors, or deployment flaws**.

Common Types of AI Bias

Type of Bias	Description	Example
Historical Bias	Bias inherent in past data	Hiring models trained on male-dominated industries favor men.
Sampling Bias	Underrepresentation of certain groups	A facial recognition model trained mostly on light-skinned faces performs poorly on darker skin tones.
Measurement Bias	Data collection errors leading to skewed predictions	Loan approval models using ZIP codes may correlate with racial demographics.

Algorithmic Bias	Bias introduced by model structure or training dynamics	A content recommendation system amplifies misinformation based on engagement metrics.

Case Study: Amazon's Biased Hiring Model

Amazon built a hiring AI trained on **10 years of resumes**, predominantly from **male applicants**. The model **penalized resumes with "women's" keywords** (e.g., "women's chess club"). This **historical bias** resulted in unfair hiring practices.

Detecting and Measuring Bias in AI Models

Bias detection requires **quantitative metrics** that evaluate disparities between groups.

1. Evaluating Dataset Bias

Checking Class Distributions

Before training, check dataset distributions to identify **imbalanced groups**.

Python (`dataset_analysis.py`)

python

```
import pandas as pd

# Load dataset

df = pd.read_csv("hiring_data.csv")


# Check distribution across genders

print(df["gender"].value_counts())


# Check average salaries across demographic
groups

print(df.groupby("gender")["salary"].mean(
))
```

If one demographic is **significantly underrepresented**, the model may produce biased predictions.

---

2. Bias Metrics for Model Evaluation

AI fairness libraries provide statistical tests to detect bias.

Key   Fairness   Metrics:
Disparate Impact Ratio – Measures if one group receives favorable outcomes significantly more than another. **Equalized Odds** – Ensures equal false positive and false negative rates across groups. **Demographic Parity** – Ensures model predictions are independent of sensitive attributes.

Using AI Fairness 360 (AIF360) to Measure Bias

python

```
from aif360.datasets import AdultDataset

from aif360.metrics import BinaryLabelDatasetMetric

# Load dataset

dataset = AdultDataset()
```

```
# Define privileged and unprivileged groups
(e.g., male vs. female)

metric = BinaryLabelDatasetMetric(dataset,
privileged_groups=[{'sex':              1}],
unprivileged_groups=[{'sex': 0}])



# Calculate bias metrics

print(f"Disparate         Impact         Ratio:
{metric.disparate_impact()}")

print(f"Statistical   Parity   Difference:
{metric.statistical_parity_difference()}")
```

A **Disparate Impact Ratio < 0.8 or > 1.25** indicates significant bias.

Bias Mitigation Strategies

1. Data Preprocessing: Rebalancing the Dataset

If certain groups are underrepresented, we can **resample** the dataset to achieve a balanced distribution.

python

```python
from sklearn.utils import resample

# Separate majority and minority groups

female_samples = df[df["gender"] == "female"]

male_samples = df[df["gender"] == "male"]


# Upsample minority class

female_upsampled = resample(female_samples, replace=True, n_samples=len(male_samples))


# Merge balanced dataset

balanced_df = pd.concat([male_samples, female_upsampled])

balanced_df.to_csv("balanced_hiring_data.csv", index=False)
```

This approach ensures **fair representation** during model training.

---

2. Algorithmic Fairness: Debiasing AI Models

Reweighing Training Data

The **Reweighing** technique assigns **higher weights to underrepresented groups**, making the model less biased.

python

```
from         aif360.algorithms.preprocessing
import Reweighing

# Apply reweighing

rw                                          =
Reweighing(unprivileged_groups=[{'sex':
0}], privileged_groups=[{'sex': 1}])

balanced_dataset                            =
rw.fit_transform(dataset)
```

This method **adjusts the importance of training samples** without changing the original dataset.

3. Post-Processing: Adjusting Model Predictions

Equalized Odds Postprocessing

Ensures similar **false positive and false negative rates** across different groups.

python

```
from       aif360.algorithms.postprocessing
import EqOddsPostprocessing

eq_odds                                    =
EqOddsPostprocessing(privileged_groups=[{'
sex':   1}],   unprivileged_groups=[{'sex':
0}])

eq_odds.fit(dataset, dataset)

transformed_dataset                        =
eq_odds.transform(dataset)
```

This technique **adjusts final predictions** to reduce unfair disparities.

Fairness in AI Pipelines with LangGraph and LangChain

LangGraph and LangChain can incorporate **fairness-aware AI workflows** by integrating **bias-detection modules** before model predictions.

1. Integrating Bias Detection into AI Pipelines

A **LangGraph pipeline** can analyze bias before generating AI responses.

python

```
from langgraph.graph import StateGraph

from aif360.metrics import BinaryLabelDatasetMetric

def bias_check_step(dataset):

    metric = BinaryLabelDatasetMetric(dataset,
privileged_groups=[{'sex': 1}],
unprivileged_groups=[{'sex': 0}])

    if metric.disparate_impact() < 0.8 or
metric.disparate_impact() > 1.25:
```

```
        return "Bias Detected"

    return "Proceed"


graph = StateGraph()

graph.add_step("bias_check",
bias_check_step)
```

This **prevents biased AI outputs** before deployment.

---

2. Implementing Ethical AI Decision-Making in LangChain

LangChain-powered AI agents should **consider fairness constraints** when making decisions.

python

```
from langchain.chains import LLMChain

from langchain.llms import OpenAI


llm = OpenAI(model_name="gpt-4")
```

```python
prompt = """

Analyze the hiring data and ensure no group
is disadvantaged.

Return an unbiased hiring recommendation.

"""



chain = LLMChain(llm=llm, prompt=prompt)

response = chain.run(input_data)

print(response)
```

By **explicitly instructing AI to ensure fairness**, we can create more ethical workflows.

10.2 Security Risks and Best Practices

As AI systems become more integrated into **critical applications**—ranging from finance and healthcare to autonomous systems and cybersecurity—**security vulnerabilities** pose increasing risks. AI workflows, particularly those built using

LangGraph and LangChain, must be designed to resist threats such as **data poisoning, adversarial attacks, model theft, and unauthorized access.**

This chapter explores:

Common security threats in AI workflows and how they manifest in real-world applications. **Secure design principles** to mitigate security risks. **Techniques for implementing authentication, access control, and encryption** in AI pipelines. **Best practices for protecting AI models from adversarial manipulation and data breaches. Step-by-step implementation of security-enhanced AI workflows using LangGraph and LangChain.**

By the end of this chapter, you will have a **comprehensive understanding of security risks in AI** and practical strategies to **build secure and resilient AI applications.**

---

1. Understanding Security Risks in AI Workflows

AI models operate on **massive datasets, complex pipelines, and third-party APIs**, making them susceptible to numerous threats.

1.1 Key Security Threats

Security Threat	Description	Example
Data Poisoning	Injecting malicious data to corrupt AI models	An attacker manipulates training data to make a fraud detection model ignore fraudulent transactions.
Adversarial Attacks	Crafting inputs to deceive AI models	An image classifier misidentifies an object due to adversarial perturbations.
Model Inversion Attacks	Extracting sensitive data from AI models	An attacker reconstructs private training data from a deployed model.

Unauthorized API Access	Exploiting insecure API endpoints	A hacker queries an LLM API with malicious inputs to leak sensitive information.
Model Theft	Stealing proprietary AI models	An attacker queries an AI model extensively to recreate its functionality.
Data Leakage	AI models unintentionally revealing confidential data	A chatbot trained on private conversations exposes user data in responses.

2. Securing AI Pipelines: Core Best Practices

2.1 Secure Data Handling

Sanitizing Training Data

To prevent **data poisoning**, ensure that training data is **validated, cleaned, and monitored** for anomalies.

python

```python
import pandas as pd

# Load dataset
df = pd.read_csv("training_data.csv")


# Detect duplicate and anomalous entries
df = df.drop_duplicates()

df = df[df["label"].notna()]    # Remove missing labels


# Validate against known patterns
df = df[df["text"].str.match(r"^[a-zA-Z0-9\s,.\-!?]*$")]
```

```python
df.to_csv("sanitized_data.csv",
index=False)

print("Data sanitized and saved.")
```

This process **prevents injection of malicious training samples**.

2.2 Authentication and Access Control in AI APIs

AI applications often expose **APIs for model inference**, making them **potential attack surfaces**. Implement **API authentication and access control** to prevent unauthorized usage.

API Key Authentication with FastAPI

python

```python
from fastapi import FastAPI, Depends,
HTTPException

from fastapi.security.api_key import
APIKeyHeader

app = FastAPI()

API_KEY = "your_secure_api_key"
```

```python
api_key_header = APIKeyHeader(name="X-API-
KEY")


def verify_api_key(api_key:    str    =
Depends(api_key_header)):

    if api_key != API_KEY:

        raise
HTTPException(status_code=403,
detail="Invalid API Key")

    return api_key


@app.get("/secure-endpoint")

def secure_function(api_key:    str    =
Depends(verify_api_key)):

    return   {"message":   "Secure   access
granted"}
```

Ensures only authorized requests can interact with the AI
model. **Prevents unauthorized API scraping** for model theft.

2.3 Encrypting AI Model Artifacts

Model files stored in **S3, databases, or on-premise** are vulnerable to theft. Encrypt models before storage.

Encrypting a Model with Fernet (AES-based Encryption)

python

```python
from cryptography.fernet import Fernet

# Generate and store key securely

key = Fernet.generate_key()

cipher = Fernet(key)


# Encrypt model file

with open("model.pkl", "rb") as file:

    encrypted_data                      =
cipher.encrypt(file.read())
```

```python
with open("model_encrypted.pkl", "wb") as
file:
    file.write(encrypted_data)


print("Model encrypted successfully.")
```

Protects models from **unauthorized access and tampering**.

---

3. Protecting AI Models from Adversarial Attacks

3.1 Detecting Adversarial Inputs

Using Adversarial Robustness Toolbox (ART)

ART helps detect adversarial perturbations in AI inputs.

python

```python
from art.estimators.classification import
PyTorchClassifier

from     art.attacks.evasion     import
FastGradientMethod
```

```python
import torch

# Define AI model (example)

model = torch.nn.Linear(10, 2)


# Wrap model for ART analysis

classifier                        =
PyTorchClassifier(model=model)


# Generate adversarial examples

attack = FastGradientMethod(classifier)

adversarial_samples               =
attack.generate(x=test_data)


print("Adversarial   samples   detected:",
adversarial_samples)
```

Identifies **malicious inputs before inference**, preventing exploitation.

3.2 Implementing Adversarial Defenses

To make models more **robust**, apply **adversarial training**—training AI models with adversarial examples.

python

```python
# Train AI model with adversarial examples
for epoch in range(epochs):
    for batch in train_loader:
        adversarial_batch                    =
attack.generate(x=batch)


model.train_on_batch(adversarial_batch,
batch_labels)
```

Increases **resistance to adversarial perturbations**.

4. Securing AI Workflows with LangGraph and LangChain

4.1 Implementing Secure Execution in LangGraph

LangGraph enables **secure AI pipeline execution** by incorporating **verification steps** before executing AI tasks.

python

```python
from langgraph.graph import StateGraph

def verify_input(data):

    if "<script>" in data["text"]:    #
Prevent XSS injections

        return "Rejected"

    return "Proceed"



graph = StateGraph()

graph.add_step("input_verification",
verify_input)
```

Prevents **malicious input injections**.

4.2 Secure Model Invocation in LangChain

LangChain AI agents **must ensure confidential data is not exposed** in outputs.

Sanitizing AI Outputs

python

```
from langchain.chains import LLMChain

from langchain.llms import OpenAI


def sanitize_output(response):

    blocked_terms    =    ["confidential",
"password"]

    for term in blocked_terms:

        response = response.replace(term,
"[REDACTED]")

    return response


llm = OpenAI(model_name="gpt-4")
```

```
chain              =              LLMChain(llm=llm,
output_parser=sanitize_output)

response    =    chain.run("Summarize    this
classified document.")

print(response)
```

Prevents **data leakage through AI-generated responses**.

10.3 Responsible AI Deployment

As AI systems become integral to businesses and society, deploying them responsibly is critical. A responsible AI deployment ensures that models are ethical, secure, transparent, and aligned with human values. This chapter explores key principles, best practices, and practical strategies for integrating responsible AI deployment into LangGraph and LangChain workflows.

We will cover:

- The core principles of responsible AI deployment
- Transparency, explainability, and accountability
- Monitoring AI systems in production
- Compliance with ethical and legal frameworks
- Implementing guardrails to prevent harmful AI behavior

1. Principles of Responsible AI Deployment

Responsible AI deployment is built on several foundational principles:

1.1 Fairness and Bias Mitigation

AI models must be designed to minimize bias and promote fairness. This involves:

- **Identifying and auditing bias** in training data and model predictions.
- **Using diverse datasets** to prevent underrepresentation of certain groups.
- **Implementing fairness-aware algorithms** that mitigate discriminatory patterns.

Example: Bias Detection in NLP Models Using AI Fairness 360 to analyze bias in a language model:

Python

python

```
from        aif360.datasets        import
BinaryLabelDataset

from        aif360.metrics        import
BinaryLabelDatasetMetric
```

```
# Load dataset

dataset    =    BinaryLabelDataset(df=data,
label_names=['prediction'],
protected_attribute_names=['gender'])


# Check bias

metric = BinaryLabelDatasetMetric(dataset,
privileged_groups=[{'gender':        1}],
unprivileged_groups=[{'gender': 0}])

print("Disparate                   impact:",
metric.disparate_impact())
```

This example checks whether gender bias exists in predictions, helping mitigate discrimination.

1.2 Transparency and Explainability

AI models should be interpretable so that users can understand and trust their decisions. Techniques include:

- **SHAP (SHapley Additive Explanations)** for feature importance.

- **LIME (Local Interpretable Model-Agnostic Explanations)** for local decision interpretation.
- **Model cards** to document AI system behavior.

Python

python

```
import shap

explainer = shap.Explainer(model.predict, data)

shap_values = explainer(data_sample)

shap.plots.waterfall(shap_values[0])
```

This code snippet generates a SHAP explanation for a model prediction, providing insights into how decisions are made.

1.3 Accountability and Human Oversight

AI systems should not operate autonomously without human oversight. Implement:

- **Human-in-the-loop (HITL)** review processes.
- **Audit logs** for decision traceability.
- **Intervention mechanisms** to correct incorrect model outputs.

2. Monitoring AI Systems in Production

Ensuring AI models perform reliably in real-world scenarios requires continuous monitoring.

2.1 Model Performance Drift Detection

AI models degrade over time due to changes in data distributions. Regularly monitor drift using:

- **Statistical tests** (e.g., KL divergence, Jensen-Shannon divergence).
- **Concept drift detectors** like `River` or `EvidentlyAI`.

Python

python

```python
from evidently import Report

from evidently.metrics import DataDriftTable


report = Report(metrics=[DataDriftTable()])
```

```
report.run(reference_data=train_data,
current_data=new_data)

report.show()
```

This generates a drift report comparing new data with training data.

2.2 Explainable Failure Analysis

Detecting and debugging AI failures ensures responsible deployment:

- **Logging misclassifications** for review.
- **Tracking model confidence scores** to detect anomalies.
- **Using counterfactual explanations** to understand AI failures.

2.3 Human Feedback Loops

Incorporating human feedback helps refine AI models:

- **Reinforcement learning from human feedback (RLHF)** to improve performance.
- **User feedback mechanisms** in AI applications.
- **A/B testing** to evaluate new model versions before full deployment.

3. Compliance with Ethical and Legal Frameworks

AI deployment must adhere to regulatory and ethical standards.

3.1 GDPR and Data Privacy

Under GDPR and similar laws:

- **Data minimization**: Use only necessary data.
- **Right to explanation**: Users should understand AI decisions.
- **Consent and transparency**: Clearly communicate AI usage.

Data Anonymization Example Python

python

```python
from faker import Faker

fake = Faker()

data["user_id"] = [fake.uuid4() for _ in range(len(data))]
```

This anonymizes sensitive user data, helping maintain privacy compliance.

3.2 AI Ethics Frameworks

Follow industry standards for responsible AI:

- **IEEE Ethically Aligned Design**
- **OECD AI Principles**
- **NIST AI Risk Management Framework**

3.3 Preventing AI Misuse

- **Access controls** to restrict AI system usage.
- **AI red-teaming** to stress-test AI against adversarial attacks.
- **Prevention of misinformation** in AI-generated content.

---

4. Implementing Guardrails in LangGraph and LangChain

LangGraph and LangChain can enforce responsible AI through structured workflows.

4.1 Implementing Content Moderation

Use OpenAI's moderation API to filter harmful content in AI responses.

Python

python

```python
from openai import OpenAI

def moderate_text(input_text):

    response                      =
OpenAI.Moderation.create(input_text)

    return
response['results'][0]['flagged']


input_text = "Some inappropriate content"

if moderate_text(input_text):

    print("Content        flagged        for
moderation.")
```

4.2 Logging and Auditing AI Decisions

Integrate logging for accountability: **Python**

python

```python
import logging

logging.basicConfig(filename="ai_decisions
.log", level=logging.INFO)
```

```python
def log_decision(input_text, ai_output):

    logging.info(f"User          Input:
{input_text} | AI Output: {ai_output}")



log_decision("User   query",   "AI-generated
response")
```

This logs AI interactions for traceability.

4.3 Implementing Role-Based Access Control

Restrict AI usage based on user roles: **Python**

python

```python
from flask import Flask, request

app = Flask(__name__)


roles = {"admin": ["full_access"], "user":
["limited_access"]}
```

```python
def check_access(role, permission):

    return permission in roles.get(role,
[])


@app.route("/api", methods=["POST"])

def api():

    user_role                        =
request.headers.get("Role")

    if    not    check_access(user_role,
"full_access"):

        return "Access Denied", 403

    return "AI Response"

app.run()
```

This ensures that only authorized users can access AI functionalities.

Chapter 11: Future of AI Workflows with LangGraph and LangChain

The field of AI automation is evolving rapidly, with new trends shaping the way AI workflows are designed, scaled, and optimized. As LangGraph and LangChain continue to grow in capabilities, developers and organizations must stay ahead by adopting emerging best practices, leveraging enterprise-grade scaling strategies, and preparing for the next wave of AI-driven development.

In this chapter, we will explore:

- Key trends in AI automation and workflow orchestration
- Strategies for scaling AI workflows to meet enterprise demands
- Future advancements in AI-driven development and what to expect next

By understanding these aspects, developers can ensure that their AI workflows remain robust, scalable, and future-proof.

11.1 Emerging Trends in AI Automation

AI automation is undergoing a rapid transformation, driven by advances in large language models (LLMs), multi-agent systems, real-time orchestration, and self-improving AI workflows. As businesses increasingly rely on AI to enhance efficiency and

353

decision-making, AI workflows are evolving to become more **autonomous, scalable, and adaptable**.

This section explores key emerging trends in AI automation, including:

- The rise of **autonomous AI agents** and **multi-agent collaboration**
- The shift toward **self-learning AI systems**
- The adoption of **real-time event-driven AI architectures**
- The role of **explainability and governance in AI automation**

Each trend is examined through technical insights, practical implementations, and real-world applications to help developers build cutting-edge AI workflows with **LangGraph and LangChain**.

11.1.1 Autonomous AI Agents and Multi-Agent Collaboration

Traditional AI workflows follow a predefined sequence of tasks. However, **autonomous AI agents** are reshaping automation by enabling **dynamic reasoning, decision-making, and task execution** without human intervention.

What Are Autonomous AI Agents?

Autonomous AI agents are self-governing entities that can:

- Perceive their environment (data, user inputs, external sources)
- Make decisions based on objectives
- Adapt strategies based on real-time feedback

With **LangGraph**, these agents can be structured as **graph-based workflows**, enabling coordination between multiple agents for complex tasks.

Multi-Agent Workflows in LangGraph

A multi-agent system consists of **specialized AI agents** that collaborate within a workflow. For example, in an AI-driven research assistant, different agents handle:

1. **Data retrieval** (gather information from web or databases)
2. **Analysis** (extract key insights)
3. **Summarization** (convert findings into structured responses)

Example: Implementing a Multi-Agent Workflow

Python

python

```python
from langgraph.graph import StateGraph

from langchain.chat_models import ChatOpenAI

from langchain.tools import WikipediaQueryRun

from langchain.schema import AIMessage, HumanMessage


# Initialize LLM and tools

llm = ChatOpenAI(model="gpt-4")

wiki_tool = WikipediaQueryRun()


# Define agent functions

def research_agent(input):
    search_result = wiki_tool.run(input["query"])
    return {"research": search_result}
```

```python
def analysis_agent(input):

    analysis                            =
llm([HumanMessage(content=f"Analyze:
{input['research']}")])

    return {"analysis": analysis.content}


def summarization_agent(input):

    summary                             =
llm([HumanMessage(content=f"Summarize:
{input['analysis']}")])

    return {"summary": summary.content}


# Define workflow

graph = StateGraph()

graph.add_node("research", research_agent)

graph.add_node("analysis", analysis_agent)

graph.add_node("summarization",
summarization_agent)
```

```
graph.add_edge("research", "analysis")

graph.add_edge("analysis",
"summarization")


graph.set_entry_point("research")

graph.compile()
```

This approach enables autonomous agents to **dynamically collaborate** within a structured AI workflow.

Real-World Applications of Multi-Agent AI

- **Customer Support Automation:** AI agents handling inquiries, issue resolution, and escalation.
- **Financial Market Analysis:** AI-driven research, sentiment analysis, and trade recommendations.
- **Legal Document Processing:** AI agents analyzing legal cases and summarizing rulings.

11.1.2 Self-Learning AI Systems

A major trend in AI automation is the ability for systems to **learn from user feedback and real-world interactions**. Instead of static rule-based decision-making, modern AI workflows are evolving into **adaptive systems**.

How Self-Learning AI Works

Self-learning AI pipelines leverage:

- **Reinforcement Learning with Human Feedback (RLHF)** to refine responses
- **Automated model fine-tuning** to incorporate new patterns
- **Memory-enhanced AI** that retains past interactions

Example: Incorporating User Feedback into AI Responses

Python

python

```python
feedback_store = {}

def ai_response_with_feedback(user_input,
feedback=None):
```

```
    response                          =
llm([HumanMessage(content=user_input)]).co
ntent

    if feedback:

        feedback_store[user_input]       =
feedback

    return response


# Example usage

response                              =
ai_response_with_feedback("Explain
LangGraph")

print(response)
```

Here, AI responses can be fine-tuned based on user feedback, enabling continuous improvement.

Real-World Applications of Self-Learning AI

- **Personalized Chatbots:** AI assistants adapting to individual user preferences.

- **Fraud Detection:** Continuous refinement of fraud detection models based on new attack patterns.
- **Healthcare AI:** AI models learning from doctor feedback to improve diagnostic accuracy.

11.1.3 Real-Time AI Orchestration and Event-Driven Workflows

Traditional AI workflows process batch-based data, but modern automation demands **real-time decision-making**.

Event-Driven AI Architectures

Real-time AI orchestration is driven by:

- **Streaming data processing** (Kafka, Apache Flink)
- **Event-based triggers** (AWS Lambda, Webhooks)
- **Dynamic AI decision-making**

This enables AI workflows to **react to live events** rather than relying on periodic batch jobs.

Example: AI Inference on Real-Time Data Streams

Python

python

```python
from kafka import KafkaConsumer

consumer = KafkaConsumer('ai_requests',
bootstrap_servers=['localhost:9092'])


for message in consumer:
    ai_response                      =
llm([HumanMessage(content=message.value.de
code('utf-8'))]).content

    print(f"Processed    AI    Request:
{ai_response}")
```

This setup allows AI models to **process incoming data streams in real time**.

Real-World Applications of Real-Time AI

- **Financial Trading AI:** Responding instantly to market fluctuations.
- **Cybersecurity Threat Detection:** AI-driven anomaly detection in network traffic.
- **Smart Manufacturing:** AI optimizing factory operations based on live sensor data.

11.1.4 Explainability and Governance in AI Automation

As AI automation becomes more widespread, organizations must ensure **transparency, fairness, and compliance** in their workflows.

Key Aspects of AI Governance

- **Explainable AI (XAI):** Making AI decisions interpretable for end users.
- **Bias Mitigation:** Identifying and reducing bias in AI models.
- **Regulatory Compliance:** Ensuring adherence to GDPR, HIPAA, and industry regulations.

Example: Generating Explainable AI Outputs

Python

python

```python
def explain_ai_decision(input_text):
    explanation = llm([HumanMessage(content=f"Explain your reasoning: {input_text}")]).content
    return explanation
```

```
print(explain_ai_decision("Why    did    you
recommend this stock?"))
```

This provides **transparent AI decision-making**, crucial for industries like **finance and healthcare**.

Real-World Applications of AI Explainability

- **AI-powered Legal Advisory:** Justifying AI-driven legal recommendations.
- **Healthcare Diagnostics:** Explaining AI-assisted medical decisions to doctors.
- **Credit Scoring Models:** Ensuring fairness in AI-based loan approvals.

11.2 Scaling AI Workflows for Enterprise Applications

As enterprises integrate AI-driven solutions at scale, the need for **highly scalable, resilient, and efficient AI workflows** becomes critical. AI applications must handle **large-scale data processing, high-concurrency inference, and real-time decision-making** while maintaining robustness and compliance.

Scaling AI workflows involves:

- **Optimizing computational efficiency** to reduce latency and improve throughput
- **Ensuring horizontal and vertical scalability** for handling enterprise workloads
- **Implementing fault-tolerant and resilient AI pipelines**
- **Leveraging distributed processing and cloud-native AI architectures**
- **Enforcing security, governance, and compliance in large-scale AI systems**

This section explores the key principles, best practices, and hands-on implementations for scaling **LangGraph and LangChain** workflows for enterprise environments.

11.2.1 Architecting Scalable AI Pipelines

AI pipelines at an enterprise level require a structured approach to handle:

- **High-volume data ingestion**
- **Parallelized processing**
- **Efficient inference execution**
- **Seamless integration with enterprise infrastructure**

Key Design Considerations for Scalable AI Workflows

1. **Modular and Decoupled Architecture**
   - Break down AI pipelines into independent, reusable components.
   - Use **event-driven architectures** to enable asynchronous processing.

2. **Microservices and API-Driven AI Workflows**
   - Deploy AI services as **containerized microservices** (Docker, Kubernetes).
   - Expose AI capabilities via **REST or gRPC APIs** for interoperability.

3. **State Management and Caching**
   - Use **stateful AI agents** when needed but leverage **caching** (Redis, Memcached) to optimize performance.

4. **Fault Tolerance and Recovery**
   - Implement **retry mechanisms** and **checkpointing** to prevent failures from disrupting AI workflows.

11.2.2 Horizontal vs. Vertical Scaling in AI Workflows

Scaling AI applications can be achieved through **horizontal scaling (scale-out)** or **vertical scaling (scale-up)**.

Horizontal Scaling (Scaling Out)

- Involves distributing AI workloads across **multiple machines or instances**.
- Utilizes **load balancing and distributed execution frameworks**.
- Ideal for **real-time, high-traffic AI applications** (chatbots, recommendation engines).

Example: Scaling AI Agents Across Multiple Nodes

Python

python

```
from          langchain.chat_models          import
ChatOpenAI

from          concurrent.futures          import
ThreadPoolExecutor


# List of AI instances

ai_models = [ChatOpenAI(model="gpt-4") for
_ in range(3)]
```

```python
def process_request(ai_model, query):

    return ai_model.predict(query)


queries = ["Analyze financial data",
"Summarize research", "Generate code"]


# Distribute requests across AI instances
with
ThreadPoolExecutor(max_workers=len(ai_mode
ls)) as executor:

    results = list(executor.map(lambda
args:             process_request(*args),
zip(ai_models, queries)))


print(results)
```

Here, AI inference is **parallelized** across multiple instances, reducing response time.

Vertical Scaling (Scaling Up)

- Involves **enhancing computational power** (more CPU, GPU, RAM) on a single machine.
- Best suited for **batch processing and complex model training**.
- Limited by **hardware constraints and cost inefficiencies**.

For **LangGraph workflows**, horizontal scaling is preferred as AI workflows often require **distributed, concurrent execution**.

11.2.3 Distributed AI Execution with LangGraph and LangChain

For enterprise-scale AI workflows, distributed execution across multiple nodes enhances **performance and reliability**.

Key Technologies for Distributed AI

- **Ray** – Parallel computing for distributed AI workflows.
- **Kafka** – Real-time streaming and event-driven AI.
- **Dask** – Scalable data processing for AI pipelines.

Example: Running AI Agents in a Distributed Environment with Ray

Python

python

```python
import ray

from langchain.chat_models import ChatOpenAI


# Initialize Ray cluster

ray.init()


# Define a distributed AI agent

@ray.remote

def distributed_ai_agent(prompt):

    llm = ChatOpenAI(model="gpt-4")

    return llm.predict(prompt)


# Run multiple AI tasks in parallel

tasks = [distributed_ai_agent.remote(f"Task {i}") for i in range(5)]
```

```
results = ray.get(tasks)



print(results)
```

This enables AI workflows to scale **dynamically** across distributed infrastructure.

Enterprise Use Cases for Distributed AI

- **Real-time fraud detection** in financial services.
- **AI-driven monitoring in cybersecurity** for detecting anomalies.
- **AI-powered content generation** in media and marketing platforms.

11.2.4 Optimizing Performance and Efficiency in AI Workflows

Scaling AI workflows requires **optimizing model performance, reducing latency, and managing compute resources efficiently**.

Best Practices for AI Performance Optimization

1. **Model Quantization and Pruning**
   - Reduce model size using **ONNX, TensorRT** for faster inference.
2. **Efficient Caching and Preprocessing**
   - Store **frequently used responses** to minimize redundant AI calls.
3. **Batch Processing for Inference**
   - Process multiple queries simultaneously to **maximize GPU utilization**.
4. **GPU Acceleration and Hardware Optimization**
   - Leverage **TPUs, GPUs, or specialized AI accelerators** for high-speed computation.

Example: Optimizing AI Inference with Batch Processing

Python

python

```python
import torch

from transformers import AutoModelForCausalLM, AutoTokenizer

# Load AI model

model_name = "gpt-4"
```

```python
tokenizer                                    =
AutoTokenizer.from_pretrained(model_name)

model                                        =
AutoModelForCausalLM.from_pretrained(model
_name)


# Batch inference

inputs = tokenizer(["Summarize AI trends",
"Explain LangGraph"], return_tensors="pt",
padding=True)

outputs = model.generate(**inputs)


# Decode responses

responses    =    [tokenizer.decode(output,
skip_special_tokens=True)   for   output   in
outputs]

print(responses)
```

By processing requests in batches, enterprises can **reduce API calls, improve efficiency, and lower costs**.

11.2.5 Security, Compliance, and Governance in Enterprise AI

Scaling AI for enterprise applications introduces challenges related to **security, privacy, and regulatory compliance**.

Key Considerations for AI Security and Compliance

1. **Data Encryption and Secure Storage**
   - Ensure **end-to-end encryption (TLS, AES-256)** for AI workflows.
2. **Access Control and Authentication**
   - Implement **OAuth, JWT, API Gateway security** for AI APIs.
3. **Bias and Fairness Audits**
   - Regularly evaluate AI models for **bias detection and ethical compliance**.
4. **Regulatory Compliance (GDPR, HIPAA, SOC 2)**
   - Adhere to industry standards for handling **sensitive AI-driven data**.

Example: Implementing Role-Based Access Control (RBAC) for AI APIs

Python

python

```python
from fastapi import FastAPI, Depends,
HTTPException

from authlib.integrations.starlette_client
import OAuth2AuthorizationCodeBearer



app = FastAPI()

oauth2_scheme                              =
OAuth2AuthorizationCodeBearer(tokenUrl="to
ken")



# Protect AI endpoint with authentication

@app.get("/ai-secure")

async def secure_ai_query(token: str =
Depends(oauth2_scheme)):

    if token != "valid_token":
```

```
    raise
HTTPException(status_code=401,
detail="Unauthorized")

    return    {"message":    "Secure    AI
Response"}
```

This ensures that only **authorized users can access enterprise AI workflows**, enhancing security.

11.3 What's Next in AI-Driven Development

The field of AI-driven development is evolving rapidly, with new advancements reshaping how developers design, build, and scale AI-powered applications. Emerging trends such as **autonomous AI agents, real-time AI pipelines, hybrid AI architectures, and self-improving AI models** are redefining workflows.

As we look ahead, several key questions arise:

- **How will AI become more autonomous in executing complex workflows?**
- **What advancements will make AI-driven development more efficient and scalable?**
- **How will new AI paradigms impact application design and enterprise adoption?**

This chapter explores **the next generation of AI development**, focusing on **emerging architectures, best practices, and the future role of LangGraph and LangChain** in AI-driven automation.

11.3.1 Autonomous AI Agents and Self-Improving Workflows

One of the most significant trends in AI-driven development is **the shift toward autonomous AI agents** capable of learning and improving over time. These agents can **plan, execute, and refine workflows** with minimal human intervention.

Key Features of Autonomous AI Agents

1. **Goal-Oriented Execution**
   - AI agents can **break down tasks into sub-goals** and execute them efficiently.
2. **Memory and Context Awareness**
   - Using **long-term memory mechanisms**, AI agents retain and use past experiences.
3. **Self-Optimization**
   - Agents analyze their performance and adjust workflows for **better efficiency**.
4. **Multi-Agent Collaboration**

- AI agents interact with each other, **delegating tasks and optimizing outcomes**.

Example: Implementing an Adaptive AI Agent with LangGraph

The following example demonstrates an AI agent that **automates workflow execution**, dynamically adjusting its steps based on real-time feedback.

Python

python

```python
from langchain.agents import AgentExecutor

from langchain.tools import Tool

from langchain.memory import ConversationBufferMemory

from langchain.llms import OpenAI


# Define AI tools

def fetch_research(query):

    return f"Researching topic: {query}"
```

```python
def summarize_data(data):

    return f"Summary: {data[:100]}..."


# Initialize tools

tools = [

    Tool(name="ResearchTool",
func=fetch_research,  description="Fetches
research data"),

    Tool(name="Summarizer",
func=summarize_data,
description="Summarizes data")

]


# Configure AI agent with memory

memory = ConversationBufferMemory()

llm = OpenAI(model="gpt-4")
```

```
agent        =        AgentExecutor(tools=tools,
llm=llm, memory=memory)


# Run an adaptive workflow

response     =     agent.run("Research     and
summarize latest AI trends")

print(response)
```

This **autonomous AI agent**:

- Selects the appropriate tool based on the task.
- Remembers previous interactions to improve future responses.
- Self-adjusts the workflow for **more efficient execution**.

Enterprise Applications:

- **Automated business intelligence** – AI agents conduct research and summarize insights.
- **Intelligent customer support** – AI agents autonomously resolve issues.
- **AI-driven project management** – AI dynamically assigns and monitors tasks.

11.3.2 Hybrid AI Architectures: Combining Symbolic AI and Deep Learning

Traditional AI applications often rely on **either rule-based symbolic AI or deep learning**. However, **hybrid AI architectures** are emerging as a more powerful approach by combining the **logical reasoning of symbolic AI with the pattern recognition of deep learning**.

Why Hybrid AI Matters

- **Improves AI explainability** – Symbolic logic helps AI provide **clear reasoning** for decisions.
- **Enhances learning efficiency** – AI models **use prior knowledge** instead of learning everything from scratch.
- **Reduces data dependency** – AI agents can work with **less training data** while maintaining accuracy.

Example: Hybrid AI for Automated Decision-Making

This example demonstrates an AI system that combines **symbolic reasoning (rules-based logic) and deep learning** for better decision-making.

Python

python

```
from langchain.chains import LLMChain
```

```python
from        langchain.prompts        import
PromptTemplate

from        langchain.chat_models        import
ChatOpenAI


# Symbolic reasoning (rule-based logic)

def rule_based_logic(input_text):

    if "urgent" in input_text:

        return "HIGH_PRIORITY"

    return "NORMAL_PRIORITY"


# Deep learning model (LLM)

llm = ChatOpenAI(model="gpt-4")

prompt                                    =
PromptTemplate(input_variables=["priority"
, "task"],

                        template="Process
task '{task}' with priority {priority}.")
```

```
chain = LLMChain(llm=llm, prompt=prompt)


# Hybrid AI workflow

task = "Analyze financial risks in stock
market (urgent)"

priority = rule_based_logic(task)

response       =       chain.run(task=task,
priority=priority)


print(response)
```

This AI system **first applies rule-based logic** to categorize tasks before **leveraging deep learning** for decision-making.

Use Cases:

- **AI-powered compliance monitoring** – AI applies business rules before analyzing risks.
- **Intelligent automation in finance** – Hybrid AI assesses market risks **faster and more accurately**.

11.3.3 Real-Time AI Pipelines for Streaming and Event-Driven Workflows

Future AI systems will increasingly operate in **real-time**, processing **continuous streams of data** instead of static inputs.

Key Technologies for Real-Time AI

- **Kafka & Pulsar** – AI workflows process **event-driven data streams**.
- **Ray & Dask** – Distributed computing for **low-latency AI inference**.
- **Vector Databases (FAISS, Pinecone)** – Fast retrieval of **semantic embeddings**.

Example: Real-Time AI Workflow with LangGraph and Kafka

This example demonstrates an AI pipeline that processes **real-time data from a Kafka stream**.

Python

python

```python
from kafka import KafkaConsumer

from langchain.chat_models import ChatOpenAI
```

```python
# Connect to Kafka stream

consumer = KafkaConsumer('ai-events',
bootstrap_servers='localhost:9092')

# AI Model

llm = ChatOpenAI(model="gpt-4")


# Process real-time AI queries

for message in consumer:

    query = message.value.decode('utf-8')

    response = llm.predict(query)

    print(f"AI Response: {response}")
```

This enables AI workflows to **analyze real-time data streams dynamically**, crucial for applications like:

- **Financial market analysis** – AI reacts to stock trends **in milliseconds**.
- **AI-powered cybersecurity** – Real-time AI identifies and mitigates threats.

11.3.4 The Future of LangGraph and AI-Driven Development

As AI-driven workflows become more complex, **LangGraph and LangChain will play a pivotal role in enabling next-generation AI development.**

Future Enhancements in LangGraph

1. **Dynamic Workflow Adaptation** – AI graphs will **self-adjust in real-time** based on changing data inputs.
2. **Multi-Agent Collaboration** – AI systems will **coordinate across multiple AI agents** for complex decision-making.
3. **Explainability & Trust in AI** – AI workflows will provide **transparent insights into decision-making**.
4. **Edge AI & Decentralized Processing** – AI models will **run at the edge** to support **low-latency applications**.

Chapter 12: Final Thoughts and Next Steps

As we reach the conclusion of this book, it is essential to reflect on the key insights gained, explore resources for further learning, and consider the next steps in expanding AI workflow projects.

The field of AI-driven development is rapidly evolving, and **LangGraph and LangChain** provide a powerful framework for building **scalable, intelligent, and automated workflows**. This chapter will:

- **Summarize the key learnings** covered throughout the book.
- **Provide resources** for deepening your understanding of AI-driven automation.
- **Offer practical guidance** on extending and scaling AI workflows in real-world applications.

Whether you are building **autonomous AI agents, real-time AI pipelines, or hybrid AI architectures**, this chapter will equip you with the next steps to continue refining and expanding your expertise.

12.1 Summary of Key Learnings

Over the course of this book, we have explored the core principles, methodologies, and practical implementations of AI workflow automation using LangGraph and LangChain. This chapter serves as a structured recap, reinforcing key takeaways and ensuring that readers walk away with a solid understanding of how to build, scale, and optimize AI-driven pipelines.

1. Fundamentals of AI Workflows

We began by introducing the foundational concepts of AI workflows, emphasizing the importance of modular, composable, and scalable architectures. Key topics included:

- The role of **graph-based AI workflows** in structuring complex tasks.
- How **LangGraph and LangChain** enable the creation of intelligent pipelines.
- The principles of **prompt engineering, retrieval-augmented generation (RAG), and multi-agent collaboration** in AI automation.

2. Building AI Pipelines with LangGraph and LangChain

Through hands-on examples, we demonstrated how to construct AI pipelines step by step. Key techniques covered:

- **Defining nodes and edges** to represent computation and data flow.
- **Integrating LLMs** with structured workflows for robust automation.

- **Using memory mechanisms** to enable stateful AI interactions.
- **Chaining multiple agents** to create dynamic, multi-step AI processes.

3. Advanced Techniques for Optimization

To enhance efficiency and performance, we explored:

- **Parallel execution strategies** to optimize response time.
- **Caching mechanisms** for reducing redundant API calls and improving cost efficiency.
- **Error handling and fallback strategies** to make AI workflows more resilient.
- **Fine-tuning and customization** to adapt models to specific enterprise needs.

4. Scaling AI Workflows for Real-World Applications

As AI adoption grows in enterprise settings, we examined best practices for scaling AI workflows, including:

- **Deploying AI systems with Kubernetes, serverless architectures, and cloud-based solutions.**
- **Data governance, monitoring, and compliance** in AI-driven automation.
- **Leveraging vector databases and hybrid search** for efficient knowledge retrieval.

5. The Future of AI Workflow Automation

Looking ahead, we discussed emerging trends that will shape the next generation of AI workflows, including:

- **Self-improving AI systems** with feedback loops and reinforcement learning.
- **Multimodal AI workflows** that integrate text, images, and structured data.
- **Ethical AI considerations** in automated decision-making.

This summary reinforces the core skills and concepts that readers have gained. In the next sections, we will provide additional resources for continued learning and practical guidance on expanding AI workflow projects.

12.2 Resources for Further Learning

As AI workflows and automation continue to evolve, staying up to date with the latest advancements is essential. This section provides a curated list of resources that will help you deepen your understanding of LangGraph, LangChain, and AI pipeline development. These resources span official documentation, research papers, online courses, books, and communities that foster collaboration and knowledge sharing.

1. Official Documentation and Tutorials

LangChain & LangGraph

- **LangChain Documentation**:
  https://python.langchain.com
    - The official reference for LangChain, including API documentation, guides, and example implementations.
- **LangGraph Documentation**: https://docs.langgraph.dev
    - Detailed documentation covering LangGraph's capabilities, from basic node-based execution to advanced multi-agent orchestration.
- **LangChain Hub**: https://hub.langchain.dev
    - A repository of LangChain templates, example projects, and integrations.

LLMs & AI APIs

- **OpenAI API Docs**: https://platform.openai.com/docs
    - Provides guidance on integrating GPT models with your applications.
- **Anthropic Claude API**: https://docs.anthropic.com
    - Covers Claude's capabilities and how to leverage it in AI workflows.
- **Google Vertex AI**: https://cloud.google.com/vertex-ai/docs

- Offers tools for building, training, and deploying AI models on Google Cloud.

---

2. Online Courses and Tutorials

AI & Machine Learning

- **Fast.ai's Practical Deep Learning for Coders** – https://course.fast.ai
  - A beginner-friendly introduction to AI model training and deployment.
- **DeepLearning.AI Specializations** – https://www.deeplearning.ai
  - A series of courses covering AI fundamentals, LLMs, and generative AI.
- **Andrew Ng's Machine Learning Course** (Coursera) – https://www.coursera.org/learn/machine-learning
  - A foundational course in machine learning with practical applications.

LangChain and AI Workflow Development

- **LangChain YouTube Channel** – https://www.youtube.com/c/LangChain
  - Video tutorials and walkthroughs of real-world use cases.

- **Building LLM Applications with LangChain** (DeepLearning.AI) – https://www.deeplearning.ai/short-courses/langchain
  - A hands-on course focused on building AI-driven applications using LangChain.

---

3. Research Papers and Industry Reports

To stay at the cutting edge of AI development, reviewing academic papers and industry reports is crucial.

- **Attention Is All You Need** – The original Transformer paper by Vaswani et al. (2017). https://arxiv.org/abs/1706.03762
- **Retrieval-Augmented Generation (RAG) for Large Language Models** – A key paper on enhancing AI responses with external data. https://arxiv.org/abs/2005.11401
- **Scaling Laws for Neural Language Models** – Analyzing how model size and compute impact performance. https://arxiv.org/abs/2001.08361

For AI trends and best practices:

- **State of AI Report** – An annual report analyzing the latest developments in AI. https://www.stateof.ai
- **McKinsey's AI Adoption Report** – Insights into how enterprises are leveraging AI at scale.

https://www.mckinsey.com/business-functions/mckinsey-analytics

---

4. Community and Discussion Forums

Engaging with AI communities provides valuable insights, troubleshooting support, and networking opportunities.

- **LangChain Discord Server**: https://discord.gg/langchain – A community of developers discussing LangChain applications.
- **Hugging Face Forums**: https://discuss.huggingface.co – Covers transformers, fine-tuning, and AI model deployment.
- **Reddit – r/MachineLearning**: https://www.reddit.com/r/MachineLearning – Discusses cutting-edge research and AI advancements.
- **Stack Overflow – AI & ML**: https://stackoverflow.com/questions/tagged/machine-learning – A place to ask and answer AI-related technical questions.
- **LinkedIn AI & ML Groups** – Networking groups focused on AI-driven development.

5. AI Open-Source Tools and Repositories

Exploring open-source projects allows you to learn from real-world implementations.

- **LangChain GitHub**:
  https://github.com/hwchase17/langchain
- **LangGraph GitHub**:
  https://github.com/langgraph/langgraph
- **Hugging Face Model Hub**:
  https://huggingface.co/models – A vast collection of pre-trained AI models.
- **FAISS (Facebook AI Similarity Search)**:
  https://github.com/facebookresearch/faiss – A tool for efficient similarity search in AI applications.
- **Ray (Scalable AI Pipelines)**: https://github.com/ray-project/ray – A framework for scaling AI workflows.

12.3 Expanding Your AI Workflow Projects

Building AI workflows with LangGraph and LangChain is only the beginning. Once you have a solid foundation, the next step is to refine, expand, and scale your AI-driven applications. This chapter explores advanced techniques, project ideas, and best practices to help you enhance your existing workflows, integrate new capabilities, and optimize performance for production environments.

---

1. Scaling AI Pipelines for Real-World Applications

As AI applications move from prototypes to production, they must handle higher volumes of requests, ensure reliability, and maintain efficiency. Scaling an AI workflow involves optimizing performance, reducing latency, and improving fault tolerance.

1.1 Parallelizing AI Tasks

AI workflows often contain multiple steps, such as data preprocessing, inference, and post-processing. By leveraging parallel execution, you can improve efficiency.

Example: Parallelizing Document Processing with LangGraph

Python:

python

```
from langgraph.graph import StateGraph
```

```python
from langchain.schema import Document


# Define a processing function

def process_document(doc: Document):

    # Simulate AI processing (e.g.,
embedding generation, classification)

    return {"content": doc.page_content,
"summary": "AI-Generated Summary"}


# Define a parallel execution workflow

graph = StateGraph()

graph.add_node("process",
process_document)

graph.set_entry_point("process")


# Sample documents

docs = [Document(page_content="First
document"), Document(page_content="Second
document")]
```

```
# Process documents in parallel

results = graph.invoke_parallel([{"doc":
doc} for doc in docs])

print(results)
```

1.2 Implementing Load Balancing for AI Requests

When serving multiple AI requests, distributing the load across multiple instances ensures better response times and avoids server bottlenecks. Load balancers such as **NGINX, Kubernetes Horizontal Pod Autoscaler (HPA)**, and **AWS Application Load Balancer (ALB)** can distribute incoming traffic across multiple AI services.

Key Techniques:

- Use **asynchronous APIs** (FastAPI, Flask with Gunicorn) for serving AI models.
- Implement **batch processing** for inference tasks (e.g., grouping requests before processing).
- Deploy **multiple model replicas** using container orchestration (Docker, Kubernetes).

2. Enhancing AI Workflows with External Integrations

2.1 Connecting AI Pipelines to External Data Sources

Many real-world applications require integrating external data sources, such as databases, APIs, or knowledge bases.

Example: Integrating a Vector Database (FAISS) with LangChain

Python:

python

```
from langchain.vectorstores import FAISS

from langchain.embeddings import OpenAIEmbeddings

# Create an embedding store

documents = ["AI is transforming industries.", "LangChain enables modular AI workflows."]

embeddings = OpenAIEmbeddings()

vector_db = FAISS.from_texts(documents, embeddings)
```

```
# Retrieve similar documents

query = "How is AI changing businesses?"

results                              =
vector_db.similarity_search(query)

print(results)
```

This approach enables efficient similarity-based retrieval for AI-enhanced search applications.

2.2 Integrating Real-Time Streaming Data (Kafka, Pub/Sub)

AI pipelines often require real-time data processing, such as fraud detection or conversational AI. Tools like **Apache Kafka**, **Google Pub/Sub**, and **AWS Kinesis** enable event-driven architectures.

Key Techniques:

- Use **event-driven triggers** to initiate AI workflows dynamically.
- Employ **message queues (Redis, RabbitMQ)** for asynchronous processing.

- Store intermediate AI results in **NoSQL databases (MongoDB, DynamoDB)** for fast retrieval.

---

3. Implementing AI Agents for Complex Workflows

LangGraph supports agent-based workflows where different components of an AI system make autonomous decisions.

3.1 Multi-Agent AI Systems with LangChain Agents

AI agents can be designed to interact dynamically, making workflows more intelligent and autonomous.

Example: Building a Research Assistant Agent

Python:

python

```
from langchain.agents import initialize_agent
from langchain.chat_models import ChatOpenAI
from langchain.tools import WikipediaQueryRun
```

```python
# Define tools

tools = [WikipediaQueryRun()]


# Create an AI agent

agent = initialize_agent(

    tools=tools,

    llm=ChatOpenAI(model="gpt-4"),

    agent="zero-shot-react-description"

)


# Query the agent

response = agent.run("Summarize the impact
of AI in healthcare.")

print(response)
```

This agent can dynamically retrieve and process external information, making it useful for research-intensive tasks.

4. Optimizing AI Workflows for Performance and Cost

4.1 Reducing Latency in AI Pipelines

Latency optimization ensures AI applications respond quickly, improving user experience.

Techniques:

- **Quantization**: Reduce model size with tools like ONNX Runtime or TensorRT.
- **Caching**: Store AI-generated responses using Redis for frequently asked queries.
- **Edge AI Processing**: Deploy lightweight models on edge devices to reduce cloud dependency.

4.2 Cost Optimization Strategies

AI workflows can be expensive, especially when using large-scale models.

Techniques:

- Use **spot instances** on AWS or GCP for cost-effective compute.

- Implement **model distillation** to reduce computational overhead.
- Store embeddings in **cheap, scalable storage (e.g., S3, BigQuery)** rather than memory-heavy in-memory solutions.

---

5. Building AI Workflows for Production

5.1 Deployment Best Practices

Deploying AI workflows involves setting up robust infrastructure to handle requests efficiently.

Steps to Deploy an AI Workflow:

1. **Containerization**: Package AI models using **Docker**.
2. **Orchestration**: Use **Kubernetes** or **AWS ECS** for scaling.
3. **Model Monitoring**: Implement **MLflow** or **Prometheus** to track AI model performance.
4. **CI/CD for AI**: Automate deployment using **GitHub Actions** or **Jenkins**.

5.2 Implementing AI Workflow Observability

Observability ensures AI workflows run reliably by tracking key performance metrics.

Essential Observability Tools:

- **Grafana + Prometheus**: Monitor AI inference latency and API uptime.
- **Sentry**: Track errors in AI workflows.
- **Elastic Stack (ELK)**: Store and analyze AI pipeline logs.

---

6. Exploring Advanced AI Applications

6.1 Real-World AI Workflow Use Cases

To expand your projects, consider integrating AI into high-impact applications:

- **AI-Powered Chatbots**: Extend LangChain-based chatbots with multimodal capabilities.
- **Autonomous Agents**: Use LangGraph to build AI-powered assistants that perform real-world tasks.
- **AI-Driven Knowledge Management**: Implement Retrieval-Augmented Generation (RAG) for enterprise search solutions.

6.2 Experimenting with Next-Gen AI Models

Stay ahead by integrating the latest AI innovations:

- **Multimodal AI**: Use models like **GPT-4-V** for processing text and images.

- **Fine-Tuning**: Train custom AI models using **LoRA (Low-Rank Adaptation)**.
- **Self-Improving AI Agents**: Implement **RLHF (Reinforcement Learning with Human Feedback)** for adaptive AI workflows.